Miracle Dog

How Quentin Survived the Gas Chamber
To Speak for Animals on Death Row

Randy Grim

foreword by
Dr. Jane Goodall

Alpine
Blue Ribbon Books
Loveland, Colorado

Cataloging in Publication Data

Grim, Randy.
  Miracle dog : how Quentin survived the gas chamber to speak for animals on death row /
by Randy Grim ; foreword by Jane Goodall.
     p. cm.
  Includes bibliographical references.
  ISBN 1-57779-071-5
1. Quentin (Dog) 2. Dogs--Missouri--Saint Louis--Anecdotes. 3. Grim, Randy. 4. Human-
animal relationships--Missouri--Saint Louis--Anecdotes. 5. Euthanasia of animals--Moral
and ethical aspects--United States. 6. Euthanasia of animals--Social aspects--United States.
I. Title.
  SF426.2.G75 2005
  179'.3--dc22

                                                  2004066023

This book is available at special quantity discounts for organizations and clubs
or for use as a promotion, premium, or for educational use. Write for details.

For the sake of simplicity, the terms "he" or "she" are sometimes used to identify an
animal or person. These are used in the generic sense only. No discrimination of any kind
is intended toward either sex.

Many manufacturers secure trademark rights for their products. When Alpine Publications
is aware of a trademark claim, we identify the product name by using initial capital letters.

Cover Design: Ruth Linka
Cover Photo: Donna Lochmann
Editing: Deborah Helmers
Layout: Laura Newport

3 4 5 6 7 8 9 0

Printed in the United States of America.

Contents

Acknowledgments iv

Introduction by Dr. Elliot Katz v

Foreword by Dr. Jane Goodall vii

PART ONE 1

   1. No Place Like Home 3

   2. Death Row 13

   3. The Chamber of Horrors 21

PART TWO 31

   4. Media Frenzy 33

   5. He Is All Mine 41

   6. A Star Is Born 49

   7. Poster Child 61

PART THREE 69

   8. Home at Last 71

   9. The Bottom Line 77

   10. Reaching for the Stars 85

Epilogue 93

Notes 97

Appendix A—Resources 100

Appendix B—No-Kill Organizations 101

About the Author 120

In Memory of Petey

Acknowledgments

Thanks to Mary Ellen Grim (Mom), Jenn Foster, Darrell Antalick, Melinda Roth and Dr. Elliot Katz for their love and support. Pat Matreci for her wonderful eye for grammar, Donna Lochmann for her amazing eye through the camera lens, Susan Russell for all her words of wisdom and friendship. Julie Castiglia for believing in me and the book, Betty McKinney of Alpine Publishing for making Quentin's story become a reality. Special thanks to an amazing editor, Deborah Helmers, and to my extended family—Stray Rescue of St. Louis and the amazing volunteers and staff! Thanks also to my publicist Andrew Kerman. Finally, I must give out a "woof" to my clan and a "meow" to my kitties—they are my dearest friends. And lastly, a special thank you to my incredible veterinarian, Dr. Edward Migneco.

Introduction

Having been part of the story you are about to read, I now know that miracles do come in many sizes, shapes, and forms, particularly when you are dealing with animal guardians and their wonderful animal companions. The moving story of Randy and Quentin's amazing journey attests to that, for it is a story of miracles. It is a story of survival, of guardianship, of the deepest kind of love, friendship, loyalty, and the miracle of hope. This book is a story of circumstances and coincidences so unique, so filled with compassion and humor that it will fill you with joy, hope, and love.

It is the tender, true story of Randy Grim and Quentin, two adorable and mischievous beings—one who survived a St. Louis gas chamber, the other an unlikely hero who has saved thousands of feral dogs from the mean streets of St. Louis. An amazing set of circumstances is destined to change the way untold numbers of people will see and treat the beautiful creatures with whom they share their lives. This new perspective will add immeasurably to the efforts of the caring people who work so hard to end the tragic deaths of millions of homeless animals killed each year in our nation's shelters, innocent beings who, through no fault of their own, find themselves unwanted and abandoned, condemned to death because not enough people cared or gave their plight a second thought.

For me, the story began when I read *The Man Who Talks to Dogs,* a beautiful, heart-warming book about an equally beautiful, heart-warming man, the one and only Randy Grim, President and founder of Stray Rescue of St. Louis. As I read about Randy's life and exploits, my heart filled with joy. I discovered a most gentle, honest, amazingly funny, and compassionate man, a special animal guardian, willing to overcome his fears for the welfare of others, in this case, the feral dogs of St. Louis, abandoned outcasts attempting to survive in the most dangerous and hostile world of urban decay. Their grim (small g) lives generally lasted no more than two to three years, until their unlikely savior, Randy Grim (with a capitol G) came along, bestowing love, sanctuary, and a new life to these uncared for, abused, and abandoned beings.

And so I discovered the perfect person, the perfect guardian to be honored at In Defense of Animals' 1st Annual Guardian Awards, joining our three other distinguished honorees: Dr. Jane Goodall; Genesis Awards founder Ms. Gretchen Wyler; and President of the San Francisco Board of Supervisors, Matt Gonzalez.

How well Randy fit in with our other honorees, who clearly represent the very best in all of us. For what Randy is to the feral dogs of St. Louis, Diane Fosse was to gorillas, and Jane Goodall to the endangered African chimpanzee. These are valiant people who share a common thread of benevolence, compassion, and courage—reaching out and giving hope to those desperately in need.

I am honored to introduce you to these two very special individuals, Quentin and Randy, each in their own way performing miracles. Share in their adventures; their story will fill your heart, as it has filled mine, with love and hope. Discover how you, too, can become part of their wonderful story, their miraculous journey, and how you, too, can work miracles.

Elliot M. Katz, DVM

Founder and President of In Defense of Animals

Internationally known and respected leader in the animal welfare movement

Randy and Quentin with Jane Goodall, Dr. Elliot Katz, Wendy Malick and Gretchen Wyler at the 2004 Guardian Awards.

Foreword

As I travel around the world 300 days a year, I meet many wonderful and inspirational people: royalty and heads of state, actors, sports stars and pop stars, leading scientists, outstanding teachers, great humanitarians.

And then, one evening in Hollywood, I met one of the most special of all the celebrities on my list. I met Quentin. As I knelt down and looked into his eyes, and felt the warmth of his little body, I was deeply moved. Quentin, the Wonder Dog, was delivered, innocent of crime, to a canine extermination camp. And yet there he was—intensely, vividly alive from the tip of his cold, black, and very inquisitive nose to the end of his joyful tail. The days of miracles are not over, after all.

Dogs have always been very special to me. Most people assume that my favorite animal is a chimpanzee. Chimpanzees are so like humans that, while there are indeed individuals I love, there are many who are not very nice at all, and some whom I actually dislike. I don't think of them as animals, but as chimpanzee beings, just as I think of human animals as human beings. And then there are these marvelous dog beings. I have shared my life, my joys and sorrows, hopes and fears, with a series of dogs. My very best friend during the years of my childhood and adolescence was Rusty. He was a spaniel-sized mutt, extraordinarily intelligent, and he went everywhere with me.

When, years later, I went to Cambridge University to write a doctoral dissertation on the results of my first year of chimpanzee studies, I had no degree of any kind. I was reprimanded by certain erudite professors for giving my chimpanzees names instead of numbers and was informed that only humans had personalities, minds and emotions. But thanks to Rusty, who had taught me so much about the basics of animal behavior, I knew this was not true. Rusty helped me to stand firm, to stick to my principles, to defy the simplistic, reductionist attitude towards animals that was widespread among ethologists in the early sixties.

A dog really is "Man's best friend" (and a child's and a woman's!). Dogs protect us and our belongings, herd our livestock, help find and rescue lost people, guide the blind. They help cure sick people, cheer up the elderly, console the lonely, and give love to the unloved. Sadly, only too often, "Man" turns out not to be Dog's best friend at all. As I travel around the world I see so much abuse of dogs. People buy and discard dogs, give them as presents to those who cannot care for them, leave them tied up on chains in the heat and the cold, shut them up for hours and hours on end, set them against each other in the ring, breed them in shameful "puppy mills," sell them to people who do not understand them and cannot possibly care for them—the list goes on. There are streets full of stray dogs, sick and starving. It is something we have come to expect in certain parts of the developing world where people also are sick and starving. But it shouldn't happen, should it, on the streets of the developed world? Yet it does. In the developing world such dogs are often shot. In the towns and cities of America they are rounded up and put in pounds, in shelters. Some of them are sold to medical research labs where they may undergo horrendous experiments. Many of them are killed by lethal injection, even by gas. This book uncovers so much of the cruelty that goes on behind the scenes in the so-called "civilized" world.

Fortunately, there is also a great deal of compassion, and many people exist who love dogs even as dogs love us. And there are some who truly can claim to be "Dog's best friend." The evening I met the very special Quentin, had dinner in the same room, and delighted in his presence, I also met the very special Randy Grim. Quentin's special-ness is the miracle of his survival. Randy's special-ness is his tireless, superhuman efforts to rescue abused, starving, sick, and homeless dogs and give them a second chance. His efforts, over the years, have made a huge difference in the lives of countless abandoned dogs. And now Randy has found Quentin. It must have been written in the stars, that meeting. What a team they make: Quentin and Randy, dog and man, partners in a campaign by In Defense of Animals to fight cruelty and ignorance. Quentin is outgoing, he loves the limelight and he gently leads the less attention-seeking Randy with him. Without Randy, Quentin might have ended up back in the gas chamber. Without Quentin, Randy would have lost the greatest "spokes-dog" for his cause. People love miracles and they love heroes. Quentin's very existence is a miracle. Randy is nothing if not heroic.

Jane Goodall, PhD, DBE
Founder—the Jane Goodall Institute
United Nations Messenger of Peace

PART ONE

ONE

No Place Like Home

MY BEDROOM IS FINALLY GOING TO SEE SOME ACTION.
But it's not what you're thinking. A photographer is on his way over—again, no,
it's not what you are thinking. He is shooting pictures on my bed for a national calendar, and *NO*, it's not what you are thinking. The subject is going to be my famous
kid, Quentin, the Basenji mix, the dog of miracles.

My bedroom is a cross between *Out of Africa* and *Scooby Doo*. A mosquito net
hangs over the bed and pictures of monkeys cover the walls. The furniture is all
Tahitian: lots of bamboo. And I have five dogs, to boot; sagebrush has nothing on
hairballs the size of basketballs. In a panic, I grab a fistful of Swiffer dusters and
begin frantically chasing the tumbleweeds back and forth across the floor. I make
up a fresh bed with its crowning glory—a handmade African quilt covered with ele-
phants—that I think will bring out the beauty of Quentin's eyes, as brown and large
as a deer's.

Fox 2 News reporter Paul Schankman has been following Quentin and me
around for months, and Paul will be at the calendar shoot as well, filming it for Fox.
My life has changed dramatically over the last few months. I now have two jobs.
One is running the organization I founded, Stray Rescue of St. Louis. Stray
Rescue's sole purpose is to rescue stray animals in need of medical attention,
restore them to health, and place them in loving adoptive homes.

My other, newer job is being the spokesperson, manager, and factotum for
Quentin. As far as I know, I am the only person on the planet who is employed by
a year-old Basenji mix. Quentin's claim to fame is miraculous, bizarre, and encouraging. He is the only dog in the country known to have survived a trip to the gas
chamber. He lived to tell his tale.

As I wait for Fox and Starpooch I check my e-mail, and the more glamorous
and bizarre aspect of my job as Quentin's public-relations man fades. I'm hit by the
reality of what my life was like before Quentin came. In my inbox are a handful of

messages about a dog who's loose on the streets at this very moment. Now that I'm "the man who talks to dogs"—the title of the book that was written about street dogs and how I try to save them—frantic e-mails and phone calls like these are a daily part of my life.

My heart sinks. The stray looks close to death, but no one can get close enough to help him. Here's a surprise: he doesn't trust humans. There are degrees of "wildness" in street dogs. Some were dumped on the streets at early ages, while others were actually born in the urban wild. Those that were discarded early on may seem to be wild, but actually do have memories of human contact, and the trick is to jar those memories of trust even if they have been skewed by abuse and neglect.

Damn! He's been sighted. I have to go help him, even if it makes me late for Quent's glamour shoot. Off I go at unprecedented speed, a full forty miles per hour—I won't go any faster without a gun to the head.

My car knows the mean streets of St. Louis by heart. On the corner of Lafayette and Nebraska lies a shepherd mix in a tight ball, maybe dead. I can't see breathing. I grab a pocketful of dog treats, climb out of my car, and slowly, gingerly, approach the lifeless mutt.

"Hey boy, I'm here to help you. Are you alive?"

He lifts his head and stares me down. I can almost see the wheels turning in his head, forming a plan of escape. Injured and now officially pissed off that I am even there, he growls and then lashes out to bite me. I hear his jaws snap. But I don't leave; instead I squat down to his level, avoiding eye contact. Taking advantage of the fact that I am staying put, he rockets up and starts to run. The poor guy is running on three legs; his one usable back leg has an open wound the size of a dinner plate, exposing muscles, tendons and bone. *Good God.* I gasp in disbelief and reach for my cell phone.

Animal Regulation and Stray Rescue have formed a working relationship over the years. Stray Rescue pulls dogs from death row and in return I usually get a high-speed response when I call in for assistance. I don't have my tools of the rescue trade with me and I need a net. "Please get here," I tell Rosemary Ficken, the supervisor at St. Louis Animal Regulation Center. "Quick." I stay on the dog's case at a safe distance.

Minutes pass. Containing the terrified dog is not easy. Like a scene from *Hansel and Gretel*, I leave a trail of treats to keep him near the hill where he was first spotted. It is working; he follows the trail back to the starting point. I hear diesel thunder. It's the Animal Control truck on the horizon. You can hear that truck miles away.

When they pull up there's no time for formalities. "I've kept him in this area with morsels of food, but we need the net."

"No problem, Randy." The two women go back to the truck for the net.

He's going to bolt, I keep thinking. His mangled body can't possibly take the strain, but he'll try to get away.

Against all odds, he doesn't. Before he knows it, the Animal Control workers perform their magic. "One, two, three," and the monster spider web drapes the frightened and angered shepherd.

But he thrashes like a live fish on the hot pavement and I know I have to start calming him down. Watching him biting through the netting, I have no choice but to try to stroke a part of his battered frame that isn't wounded or in pain, all the while keeping my fingers intact. I reach between his ears, stroking softly, again and again. Somehow you can transmit to dogs, by touch and by voice, that you won't hurt them, that you love them. They get it. All of them, however much they are in pain, get it. I start to talk him down.

"Hey, hey, it's okay. Your bad days are over. Just let me try to help you." I continue the stroking and whispering, repeating this mantra. As if hypnotized, he begins to relax and the growls—half pain, half panic—slowly diminish and then disappear entirely.

But the handlers are rough. Politely, I ask if I can take the pole so it will function more like a collar and leash than a choke hold. As I place it around his bloody neck, I keep the calming mantra going. He is shivering, quaking with terror. Up close, I can see that he is so beaten up that I don't know how he survived. The mantra is working. He nestles close to me as the net is pulled away, as though he has known me for a long time. I now start to walk him, trying to jar pleasant memories of all dogs' favorite pastime: *walkies.*

I pick him up and lay his broken body across the back seat of my Aztec. He contentedly curls up, happy to be safe and surrounded by kindness for the first time in a long time—or maybe, from the looks of it, for the first time ever. Through tears I name him "Titan" and whisk him off to the Vet Clinic. And then back to my other job as Quentin's overseer, though I knew Quent would understand helping out a fellow canine in need. Titan is a street dog, Quentin a turn-in. Both were unwanted.

Even if a street dog doesn't die of gunshot wounds or from being used as bait in dog fighting or from being thrown off a bridge, once he winds up in the shelter his chances for survival are the same as a turn-in's. If not adopted within five working days, there's a 100 percent chance that, even with so much love to give, they will both wind up in the gas chamber.

The doorbell rings, the world's most annoying rendition of the *Twelve Days of Christmas* that eerily resists all efforts at reprogramming. The dogs go into their howling routine, off-key. Starpooch Company calendar photographer Randy Solomon is at the door.

Starpooch is donating proceeds from the calendar sales to shelters across America, my main reason for accepting this gig on Quentin's behalf. The calendar will educate people and raise money for animal welfare organizations across the country.

Quentin enjoys all the attention—hell, he's thriving on it. As for me, a poster boy for panic disorder, camera spotlights have an effect on me roughly akin to a firing squad. Hence, I am on medication and occasionally see a shrink. I am a walking junkbox of neuroses, a man who must pop Xanax to walk through an airport, touch a public doorknob, or even drive on a highway. The shrink says I have social anxiety disorder; I say I just have a few "issues" to deal with—it sounds better to me. But I can't ignore any animal in need, no matter where they are. Saving a stray saves a part of me.

Photo by Randall Solomon.

Quentin doing his bird dog impression for the Starpooch photographer.

"Give me a while to set up in your bedroom," Solomon says. "Hope you don't mind if I move things around a bit."

"No problem. We have plenty of time," I say, my offhandedness obviously forced.

My friend and Stray Rescue employee, Jenn Foster, is with me. We decide to relax—as though I could—in the dining room until the photographer is ready for his star pooch. I tell her about my latest adventure, the rescue of Titan. Then Jenn asks a loaded question. "Wonder what Quentin's old home was like?"

I tell her there was no real way of telling. "He used to be afraid of people, skinny and sickly. That tells you all you need to know."

Information on previous pet "owners" is almost as tough to obtain as information on the previous owners of a used stereo bought at a pawnshop. Most of what I know about Quentin's sketchy biography has come from the staff at St. Louis Animal Regulation Center. How I would love to have interviewed these so-called guardians. I'd like to see, firsthand, where and how this dog lived. My big question for them would be, *Why?* The pat reasons on the generic pound form don't count.

I have a hard time using the word "owner." I prefer the term "guardian." Dr. Elliot Katz of In Defense of Animals sums it up best. "A critically important paradigm shift is occurring. It is a shift in how we humans perceive and relate to the animals we share our lives and planet with. An ever-growing number of citizens, humane societies, animal protection organizations, and legislators are replacing the language of ownership with that of guardianship, replacing the term 'owner' with that of 'guardian.' Owners buy and sell. Guardians adopt and rescue." [1]

Similarly, many animal rights and animal welfare people prefer the term "companion animal" to "pet." I use these words interchangeably throughout this book.

Changing the way we speak about animals can change the way we think about them. If animals are thought about as individuals, rather than as property—inert, interchangeable commodities—then that's a step toward ending the horrors millions of animals endure at the hands of people every year.

Center officials told me a few things about Quentin's former life. His name was Cain, a name he never acknowledged. His old stomping ground was south St. Louis. Life probably wasn't the greatest in this low-income, blue-collar area, but it was all he knew. Upon his arrival at the St. Louis dog pound, he was unneutered and near-ly starving, and I could count every one of his ribs.

What I learned didn't surprise me. His owners behaved as if they were exchanging a defective Christmas gift. They paid no attention to him as they filled out the necessary forms that signed away their legal rights to Cain and gave the OK for his execution. They didn't say goodbye or give Cain a kiss or a hug. What they said was, "We moved into an apartment that doesn't accept dogs." They dropped him off at the shelter like an old couch in an alley, and didn't look back as they placed him on the waiting list for death row.

It's a story we know by heart, one that's played out in every state, every day. We hear it all the time.

There are hundreds of reasons why companion animals are turned in to our nation's shelter system. Most shelters have heard every excuse known to man and dog. The most oft-used reasons range from "we're moving" to "my dog is boring."

The problems start where problems usually do: at the beginning. Shelter staff don't usually provide pet guardians with proper information about training a new dog or puppy, spaying and neutering, or solutions to behavioral problems. New guardians are not instructed how to choose the proper dog for their family and lifestyle. Nor do they often put a lot of thought into the "purchase" of a new life, a new member of the family. Frequently, dogs are chosen because they are of a particular breed—often one that's recently been featured in a popular movie, TV show, or commercial.

Our culture increasingly expects all relevant information to be handed to us: How to raise kids, how to raise dogs. Hence, when their new pet gets too big, or is too energetic, or isn't playful enough, off to the shelter he goes.

Only 12 to 14 percent of dogs nationally are adopted from shelters. Animals typically are between six and eighteen months old when they enter a shelter. Since approximately 85 percent of those in the "market" for a pet want a dog younger than one year old (and many want puppies under six months), older dogs have vir-tually no chance for adoption—their stay in the shelter is a brief interlude before death.[2]

The stigma attached to shelter animals is that they are "used goods" and must somehow be defective. It certainly doesn't help that most are mixed breeds, although purebreds do make up more than one-quarter of the nation's shelter population.[3]

There is no official data on the number of animals euthanized across the United States each year—organizations offer figures that vary between five and twelve million. Five and twelve million. Even using the mid-range estimate of 9.6 million from the American Humane Association,[4] this means that more than twenty-six thousand animals are destroyed every day, more than a thousand are destroyed every hour, and eighteen animals are destroyed every minute of every day and hour.

Adoption rates vary from city to city; the average is 25 percent;[5] not one in three animals finds a new home. Yet there are fewer than six thousand shelters for the many millions of unwanted animals.[6]

With seventy thousand puppies and kittens being born every twenty-four hours,[7] it is clear that education regarding spaying and neutering is needed. Poor funding in low-income areas doesn't help. Studies show that innovative spay/neuter programs have dramatically changed the landscape of certain areas in the United States. For example, the Shelter Reform Action Committee reports that:

- *In 1980, before the Charlotte, North Carolina, spay/neuter clinic opened, 7,814 dogs were euthanized; in 1982, 4,658 dogs were euthanized—a 40 percent decrease in killings, at a 39 percent savings for the city.*
- *In 1971, the first municipal spay/neuter clinic in the United States opened in Los Angeles, California. By 1987, animal euthanizations had dropped 58.1 percent. In spite of their success, in 1992 the clinics were closed due to various factors, including earthquakes, fires, and city riots and financial problems.*
- *In 1975, a subsidized spay/neuter clinic opened in Santa Barbara, California. Within ten years, the city shelter was euthanizing 80 percent fewer animals.*
- *In 1975, the Huron Valley, Michigan, Humane Society began subsidized neutering. By 1984, 50 percent fewer animals were entering the Huron Valley shelter.*
- *In 1976, the San Francisco, California, Society for the Prevention of Cruelty to Animals began a subsidized spay/neuter program. By 1991, the organization was no longer euthanizing dogs and cats deemed adoptable.*
- *In 1989, a low-cost spay/neuter program was begun by the Animal Foundation in Las Vegas, Nevada. Performing approximately 60 sterilizations a day, the clinic is considered a model for similar ones elsewhere in the United States.[8]*

And Best Friends Animal Sanctuary adds another encouraging story: New Hampshire began a neutering program in 1994. During the first seven years of the program, 37,210 fewer cats and dogs entered New Hampshire shelters than in the seven years before that.[9]

"He is going to be the cover shot," Solomon explains. I am the proudest dad in St. Louis.

Quentin has been running around the house, a veritable speedball, playing with the other dogs. His energy level isn't just high; it's explosive, irrepressible. He's full of joy. Solomon can't keep up with Quentin's acrobatics, which are making the rest of us laugh; I can see concern in the photographer's face that he may have a difficult subject on his hands.

"Oh, don't worry," I assure Solomon. "He has this uncanny canine ability to know when it is time to pose or educate or even fly in a plane. He will be great, you'll see." I have seen it too often now; I know that Quentin will be the consummate professional when the shoot begins.

When Solomon says, "Ready," I cue Quentin to hop up on the bed. Calm and adorable, Quentin strikes every pose Solomon wants. I turn on disco music for ambiance. Solomon's cameras are flashing; news cameras are filming. My room is a New York fashion photography studio. The subject, incongruously and gloriously, isn't a strutting human supermodel, male or female, but a mutt who made it through the gas chamber, when so many millions don't. Shelter dogs finally have a pin-up. I smile, from ear to ear. Quentin gives himself a deep backrub on the African quilt and throws the photographer a head shot.

After three more hours the entourage departs, and the house is empty except for my clan and me. The shoot was a success. I have high hopes that today will impact the fate of unwanted animals the world over, that Quentin will be a messenger of hope.

By now, his previous "owners" surely have seen him on the news, in the newspapers, or in *People* magazine. They have to be freaking out, I think, and that thought brings some twisted comfort. Quentin lies in my arms as these feelings swirl through my mind. Moving shouldn't mean the family's loyal companion gets the axe. Why didn't they look for a place that takes a dog, or even better, why didn't they place him on their own instead of so casually signing his death sentence?

Photo by Randall Solomon.

The cover shot for the Starpooch calendar.

If I knew where they lived, I would send them a calendar and a note from Quentin, giving them a piece of his doggy mind. But this is about shame and a helpless little dog. Something deep, deep inside me knows that they still wouldn't give a hoot.

My day planner is full—too many local and national television and radio shows. I decline most requests; others I accept, though I dread them. It is amazing how this one dog survived and is fast becoming America's newest canine sweetheart. I know Quentin lived for a reason, and that it isn't about the fame. I've lived long enough to know that most true heroes are unlikely ones. His bony frame and his beautiful, small, and still-frightened face can bring hope and renewal to our fractured shelter system where reams of position papers cannot. Quentin can help rid our nation of outdated, barbaric methods of euthanasia. He is a living, breathing monument to the no-kill philosophy. That is a lot to put on one dog's shoulders, not to mention those of his guardian.

Quentin, one of the many dogs considered disposable by his "family" and society.

D e a t h   R o w

WHILE QUENTIN LIVES TO TELL HIS IMPORTANT TALE, I'm not so sure I will. I'm preparing for an important dinner party, but the Miracle Dog, who one hour ago lapped up my grande vanilla mocha latte while I scoured the refrigerator for cocktail sauce, is now experiencing a caffeine rush that has him chasing imaginary rabbits back and forth across the kitchen floor.

My guests will be here any minute, and as I check on the steamed lobster tails and urgently arrange shrimp on a platter of fresh parsley, Quentin whips circles around the kitchen table, knocks over a chair, bounces up against the wall and then flings himself into midair like a dolphin diving for the sky.

"Quentin, *pleeeeease.*"

With tongue flailing, he skids across the tile and careens into a cabinet. He collects himself, unashamed, and dashes up the stairs, farting with each step. That's one of Quentin's drawbacks. He has flatulence. For some reason, doing stairs brings out the worst in him—I swear there are no letters on this keyboard adequate to describe what it sounds like.

Later that night, when an uncomfortable silence enters the dinner conversation, Quentin, barred from the dining room and pacing the stairs, provides ample background noise.

"What's that?" one of the guests asks when Quentin's rhythmic windiness marches through the silence like an oncoming tuba band.

At first I feign deafness, but it's hard to escape the sound of the offbeat baritone toots coming from the back of the kitchen.

"That would be Quentin, one of my dogs."

"Quentin? Why'd you name him Quentin?"

"Well, originally his name was Cain."

"So why Quentin?"

Why?

I find myself launching into Quentin's story, telling my guests about how he came to me, telling them about how he almost died, telling them about how he lived to steal my lattes and fart on my steps. But what I probably should have said was, "Look in his eyes. They'll tell you everything you need to know."

As you turn onto Gasconade Street, you can hear the eerie wails of dogs and the echo of true fear. At first glance the drab concrete walls and the high fencing give the appearance of a miniature San Quentin prison, but the prisoners here don't wear stripes. The sixty-two-year-old animal penitentiary is an oversized death row; its inmates have little hope for a reprieve. This is the Gasconade, the St. Louis Animal Regulation Center, the local pound for homeless and unwanted pets.

The Gasconade is a squat, ugly rectangular box with the look of a police station or a government building. Inside, the small relic of a lobby area oozes with the stench of wet dog and feces. Purebred dog charts and missing-animal posters cover the walls. Behind a glass casing sit the wardens, who have the power to buzz you into the endless halls of dogs and cats waiting, at first cluelessly and later with knowledge and trepidation, for their execution. As you approach the door to the cells, the howls grow louder and fear becomes real. The buzzer sounds and you may enter.

Cain's day came on August 5, 2003. His "owners," a husband and wife, are turning him in to the shelter. It's hard to imagine that they would move into an apartment remembering their VCR but overlooking the family dog. But it's true; the VCR is moving with the family, and Cain is brought here.

As he is led into the Gasconade, he is on high alert at the howls and moans of fear and misery and the smell of filth, fear, and something else. Something sinister and unfamiliar. He will later come to recognize it as the smell of death. His gentle, deer-like features take on the look worn by all the pound's other inmates: his eyes fill with terror and he tucks his tail beneath him. The sights and sounds of the world he once called home are gone. No more sunlight, no more fresh air.

As his papers are filled out and processed at the window, the buzzer sounds and Cain's once-outstretched ears flop down like a hound's. A towering human enters the minute lobby. The worker places a slip lead on Cain's neck. The dog doesn't know this, but if he resists, he will be put in a pole noose and dragged to

Photo by Donna Lochmann.

Animals awaiting their fate at Gasconade.

his cell. However, Cain submits. Confusion, fear, and panic saturate every fiber of his skeletal frame as he is led away from his family.

Cain's cell is 5A. This row of cells faces the St. Louis Animal Regulation Center's gas chamber.

Cain's pen holds up to five dogs. He is the fifth. The other four dogs pass the time by pacing and staring at anyone who may walk by, hoping they will be the people to take them away from this hell. Cain curls into a tight ball—in his mind, a ball of protection—as he lies on the recently hosed-down concrete floor.

As the wardens pass by, he eyes them, but nobody stops to take him out. Cain's psyche tells him to stay put. *It will get better.* But the sounds of wailing dogs tell him something different. He can see it from his pen. His eyes fixate on that chamber of horror.

In time it becomes apparent to him that he is now a witness. A blue train loaded with fellow inmates rattles up to the metallic box, and the dogs are herded inside the chamber. As they enter, some of them are wagging their tails. But only lifeless bodies come out. This is a ritual that becomes embedded into his mind as he witnesses it over and over again during the next three days.

Why?

Cain lays his head down and ponders his future as the other four-legged inmates pace the cell. He's too nervous and scared to think of being hungry, which is one small blessing. Food, which was a luxury in his previous life, is a rarity here. Low-level growls become normal, as unheard as a constant humming, while his cellmates scurry the pen in search of food morsels. A worker comes by with a hose and sprays them all down. Cain now is cold and wet. Sleeping is not an option.

Come morning, Cain stretches and for a brief second he forgets where he is. He is terrifyingly dragged back into his new reality as a train of crates, filled with barking dogs, is lined up in front of the chamber. Cain retreats into his protective fetal position and closes his brown eyes, not to slumber but to escape the moment. He raises his head from the floor, which is now covered in urine and feces, and sneezes.

Barking permeates the prison as new arrivals are marched into cells marked 5B. 7A's inmates, who were on the death train, are now herded into the gas chamber

Photo by Donna Lochmann.

The blue trolley and the chamber of horrors.

via the trolley. A fight breaks out among the newbies and the wardens scramble to break it up and separate the dogs with cold water from a nearby hose. A defeated dog lies down, blood trickling from his muzzle.

Cain looks upon the fallen soldier with empathy. His fetal position no longer comforting, Cain fearfully joins the pack and paces. He sneezes again and mucus falls to the concrete floor. 5B's pack is sick, and the newest phlegm-sounding cough has spread throughout the nearby cells. Cain wants out.

Official nationwide statistics regarding shelter animals do not exist. The American Society for the Prevention of Cruelty to Animals offers the following numbers:

- *Between eight and twelve million companion animals enter shelters nationwide every year. These are almost evenly divided between "drop-offs," those relinquished by "owners," and "turn-ins," those picked up by animal control. Perhaps nine million—60 percent of dogs and 70 percent of cats—are euthanized.*

- *Only 10 percent of the animals in shelters have been spayed or neutered, while 75 percent of pets living in permanent homes are de-sexed.*

- *About 60 percent of households in the United States have a pet; the total population of companion animals is about sixty million dogs and seventy-five million cats. The majority of pets are obtained from acquaintances and family members. Only about 10 to 20 percent of cats and dogs are adopted from shelters and rescues, about 15 to 20 percent of dogs are purchased from breeders, and 2 to 10 percent are purchased from pet shops. More than 20 percent of the people who bring a dog to a shelter adopted their animal from a shelter.*

- *It is estimated that the number of stray dogs and cats in the United States is now in the tens of millions; some estimates put the number of stray cats alone at seventy million. For every two animals who have permanent homes, there's one on the street. Many strays are lost pets that were not kept properly indoors or provided with identification, while others are the offspring of unneutered escapees.[1]*

With the tremendous numbers of animals on America's streets, animal shelters are a help in returning lost animals. Some provide low-cost spaying and neutering programs. But fewer than 2 percent of cats and only 15 to 20 percent of dogs are returned to their guardians. Most of these were identified with tags, microchips or tattoos.[2]

The dark side of America's shelters is less well known. Government shelters are run for public health reasons, meaning that they don't have a mandate to find good homes—or any homes—for the animals they take in. They just have to get rid of them.

No one knows what goes on behind closed doors. Most people don't want to know. But stories detailing inadequate feeding and watering and rough and neglectful treatment sometime come to light. One such incident occurred in 2001 at the West Gardner, Massachusetts, city animal shelter, which has since been closed. Arthur F. LeBlanc, Gardner's animal control officer since 1998, was relieved of his duties after a Rottweiler was found dead and half-eaten among two dozen other injured and hungry dogs living in filth. A health agent said conditions were adequate when he had visited the shelter about three weeks earlier, but apparently no cleaning had been done since that visit.

The situation was obscene. Filth covered the walls, food dishes, and the shelter floor. The only water available for the animals to drink was dripping from a broken heater. All that remained of the Rottweiler was his partially eaten head, spinal column, and paws. He had been cannibalized by his cellmates. Bite marks on other dogs—including at least one puppy—pointed out the likelihood of the same horrific end for them at some time in the future.

The Gardner Police department filed six counts of cruelty to animals and two counts of willful neglect on February 12, 2001, a week after the appalling conditions were discovered.[3]

In December 2003, a reporter for Miami's WSVN-TV photographed dogs during their final hours in the run at Miami-Dade animal control. The pictures show more than a dozen dogs surrounded by blood and feces. One dog is already dead—he apparently choked on his leash. Another has a leash wrapped around his belly. A puppy sits bolt upright in the midst of the filth and death, staring straight ahead.[4]

Broward County Humane Society's JoAnne Roman commented on the situation. "It's certainly inhumane for the animals both two- and four-legged. National standard in animal welfare is one animal at a time should be euthanized. Animals are extremely sensitive and perceptive and they understand fear. They can smell it. They can hear it."[5]

These types of stories are all too common in America's broken government shelter system. Conditions are usually poor, staffing inadequate, and overcrowding *the norm. The major culprits are lack of funding and staff. The St. Louis Animal Regulation Center has its share of sad tales and horror stories, but an overcrowded front lobby and rundown conditions are more obvious to the casual visitor.*

Cain paces nervously, glancing often at the injured dog in 7A. He gallops, but doesn't understand what he is running from—he is pursued by a floating, nameless fear. Coughing and sneezing interrupt his cadence, and he falls to the ground and curls up into a ball, shivering.

The train clatters up to 5A. Cain slowly lifts his head and cocks it to the left, then to the right, and his ears drop down and back. He knows.

As the wardens enter the cell, Cain hunkers in the back. The pack becomes a tangled web of panic as the steel pole with its hangman's noose reaches in. It is time for Cain to fight, to survive, to attack, to do whatever it takes to avoid capture. The first dog is noosed, and Cain watches his fellow cellmate thrash furiously to gain freedom. Eventually the dog succumbs and is pulled from the pack and put into a cage in the train.

The pole sweeps by Cain's head and attaches itself around the neck of a terrified dog to his right. Within seconds the dog is gone, never putting up resistance. Cain squirms and moves further into the corner while horror causes his little tan frame to tense up. Trembling, he defecates.

Cain knows his turn is coming. His eyes dart from one warden to the next and back to the train with its two new unwilling passengers. His only thought is *must escape.*

In a panic-driven swiftness, Cain bolts toward the partially opened door. He hits the concrete with a merciless *thud* and feels the noose tighten around his gaunt neck. Biting at the pole is useless, so Cain jerks back with all his might. His thirty pounds are no match for the heavy-hitting wardens. As he gasps for air, Cain's paws frantically scratch the cement floor, but continue to slip toward the cage. Earsplitting howls echo through the shelter.

Must escape.

Cain's undersized body slams into the cage's metal bars, and with one quick movement the noose comes off as the cage door bangs closed. Cain slinks into his fetal position and trembles. He watches as "Tuesday's" cages empty one by one. He coughs repeatedly and phlegm dangles from his nose.

Once all the cars are loaded, the train slowly begins to move. His one-way ticket to death now stamped, Cain hoists his head and watches as he passes 5B and then 6A cells, on his way to the gas chamber.

By now my dinner guests are staring at me with open mouths and have abandoned the shrimp platter altogether. I excuse myself and put the tray in the refrigerator. It's hard for me to tell Quentin's story, because it grabs me in the gut in a violent sort of way, and I have to take a break before it all gets torn out.

Quentin isn't so sentimental. In fact, he's an outright opportunist. As I sit back down at the dining room table to tell the rest of his story, I watch in amazed horror as he opens the refrigerator door with his mouth and pulls the shrimp tray off the shelf and onto the floor. He'd never done that before. I'd never seen *any* dog do that before. But then Quentin isn't just any dog.

THREE

The Chamber of Horrors

INTERRUPTED SO RUDELY BY FLATULENCE AND FALLEN shrimp, I pull out the port wine and brie cheese and arrange both carefully on the center of the table, away from the reach of unwanted hungry "paws." My guests, as if caught in the middle of a séance, have been rendered speechless as I prepare to end the Quentin saga of survival. Before we sit back down, one by one they all make sure they take advantage of this breather and use it to love on Quentin, regardless of farts. One by one they take turns loving on all my five dogs. They probably just need a dog fix, thinking of their own companion animals and how fortunate they are to have them alive and well.

Quentin tiptoes to the back of the line of adulation as if making sure the rest of the gang doesn't think he is "all that." But that is just a ploy to distract so he can sneak back and again open the fridge for another food search. This time, however, I catch him red "paw" handed.

"Hey, you—stop it now!" I hiss, hoping my friends do not hear Round 2 of the cuisine thief in action.

Quent glances at me while his jowls start to slowly release the white fridge handle. I'm afraid he may "toot" again after all that tugging, but he keeps his composure. Knowing I am on to him, he hurries back to the front of the doggy affection line with an innocent and blameless look. There are tail wags galore by the entire group as they sop up the attention.

"It really is a miracle, Randy," says one guest.

"So how did he do it? Does anyone know?" asks another.

We settle back around the table and, with our port wine in hand, we toast Quentin and his miraculous deed. I hear slurping sounds coming from the bathroom just feet away, and figure the dogs must be toasting Quent too, with toilet water—their favorite.

21

The dogs start to settle in around us at the table and lie down except Quent. He sits dignified next to me, as if he is ready to tell his tale himself. He cocks his head.

The warden reaches into the cell on the cheerless train and injects a snarling Cain with a sedative, acepromazine, which has roughly the effect of one martini. She proceeds to inject the seven other doomed passengers that have been placed with him. One can only imagine what is going through his drowsy mind about what will happen next. Cain feels the sedative rush through his veins, but it only agitates his system and causes him to stand and wobble as if he were drunk.

Fear consumes Cain. He can't tuck his tail any farther underneath himself, and he sees no escape from what is about to happen. He didn't choose to be in this animal hell. He never understood why he was here, what he'd done, or where his family and the yard he used to play in were. He waits his turn.

Spinning in circles seems to help; at least he is doing something. If he spins intoxicatingly enough, then perhaps he will magically get a reprieve and disappear from this place. Cain's cellmates seem much calmer; they succumb to the sedative. They either sit and stare depressively or lie down and await their hopeless fates.

The dogs in 7A and 7B have an unobstructed view of the gas chamber. They watch daily as the mammoth machine massacres whoever goes in, and they watch the lifeless bodies as the trolley pulls them out. These pens even have a view of the truck that transports the motionless carcasses. Staff members wonder what the dogs may be thinking or if they understand what is going on at all. Most of the employees believe the dogs know something is not right and are very much afraid.

The daunting task of executioner falls onto the shoulders of Rosemary Ficken, a supervisor and fifteen-year veteran of the Gasconade shelter. Ficken tries to spend time with each animal prior to opening the chamber door and sending them inside. Maybe those few soft, kind words will help ease their passage.

It isn't Ficken's fault that the center doesn't have the funding to rid itself of gassing, or the space to house more animals, or pens without a view of the chamber. It certainly isn't her fault that people don't take responsibility for their pets, that they don't spay or neuter them, that they don't have the commitment to be their lifetime guardians. She despises this part of her job; she must detach from her

The row of cages at Gasconade.

inner self to do it. She is consumed by sympathy every time she pulls the switch, but it is, she says, "a necessary evil" of her job.

Sedated and defeated, the inhabitants of the blue train make their way to the giant, oven-like chamber. The front door window, covered with yellow paper, prevents viewing of the inmates' final moments. Atop the large oven is an array of switches and lights—green, blue, yellow, and a clear white light that signals when the task is complete and all inside are dead.

Once the door is closed, it is dark inside, except for a small ray of light that pierces a small, square side window through which the dogs can look helplessly out at the carbon monoxide tank.

The entire trolley rolls into in the chamber. It fits like a glove. The inmates are secure; the metal door is shut. No last rites are given here. There are no witnesses and no stays of execution. The switch is turned on, and the large green tank pumps its deadly contents into the tiny room.

Cain watches his fellow inmates slowly succumb to the fatal gas, falling to the metal floor. He fights to survive, and waits for a miracle. No miracle ever has spared

Photo by Donna Lochmann.

The "all clear" light that signals when the killing is complete.

the lives of any of the 4,000-plus victims of the past year. In fact, no miracles at all have occurred in the facility's sixty-two-year history.

I will not die. I will not fall.

Cain stares out of the small side window. Five minutes pass, and one by one, his companions perish around him. There is no room to stand except on top of the fallen victims. Cain remains strong. Ten minutes pass. He hears nothing except the sound of his own breathing. Fifteen minutes pass.

He is still standing as pure oxygen is pumped into the chamber. The alarm sounds, the white light glows, and the door opens.

Bill Baskerville of the Associated Press wrote about the horrors of the gas chamber in Richmond Virginia's Daily Press *in June 2002:*

> *Mary Ellison remembers the scene vividly: Several dogs were placed in a chest freezer converted into a gas chamber. The lid, with a viewing window, was closed and the carbon monoxide in a tank next to the chamber was turned on. "There was a lot of barking, growling, crying, beating on the door trying to get out" as they were poisoned, the animal control officer said. The animals were gassed at a public pound Ellison visited in Virginia eight years ago. Today, carbon monoxide chambers—some of them jerry-built metal boxes—are still widely used in the United States to kill unwanted animals, most of them strays picked up by animal control.*

Many localities refuse to allow the public or press to watch gassings, even in Virginia, which permits press and public witnesses for human executions. Chesterfield and Henrico counties in suburban Richmond rejected a reporter's recent requests to view the use of their gas chambers. A week later Henrico, citing longtime pressure from animal rights groups, switched to lethal injection of sodium pentobarbital.

Police Maj. Warner W. Williams said Chesterfield favors gas because sodium pentobarbital is a controlled substance that must be kept locked up. It requires two people to use, one to restrain the animal and one to give the injection, and there is the possibility of an accidental needle stick, he said. Most animal welfare groups and the American Veterinary Medical Association recommend intravenous injection of sodium pentobarbital for the euthanasia of companion animals. The drug, used by most private shelters and veterinarians, produces rapid anesthesia and death. Gassing is "like a dark, dirty secret that no one wants exposed," said Jeanne Bridgforth, an animal welfare activist who launched a campaign last month to rid Virginia of its twenty-six gas chambers. Even though killings are performed at taxpayer expense, the public pounds are "doing something they don't want anyone else to see," she said.

The Humane Society of the United States estimates that four million to five million unwanted dogs and cats are euthanized annually in the United States, but it has no breakdown by method. At least three states— California, Maryland and Tennessee—have banned carbon monoxide gassing. "The easier that an animal can transition to death is helpful psychologically" to people and animals, said Tennessee's state veterinarian, Dr. Ronald Wilson. Tennessee had another reason for banning gas chambers: An employee of an animal shelter in Chattanooga died in March 2000 after being overcome by carbon monoxide used to euthanize dogs. Officials said the man apparently failed to clear the gas out of the chamber.

The American Veterinary Medical Association says carbon monoxide "is extremely hazardous for personnel" because it is highly toxic and difficult to detect and that it can be "extremely flammable and explosive." Workers who euthanize animals by injection or gas often report nightmares, flashbacks, sleep disorders, obsessive thinking and clinical depression, experts say.

Chesterfield County authorities believe gassing is less stressful than lethal injection for people who euthanize animals regularly, Williams said. "It's effective. It's humane. The animal goes to sleep," he said. It's also cheaper, said Ruth First of the American Society for the Prevention of Cruelty to Animals, a New York-based humane organization that recommends injection. She did not have comparative figures but said ASPCA officials over the years have determined carbon monoxide gassing to be less costly than sodium pentobarbital. People for the Ethical Treatment of Animals disputed that. If a municipal pound follows all of the veterinary medical association's guidelines, gassing is more expensive, said PETA's Daphna Nachminovitch.

Some localities kill animals with carbon monoxide from internal combustion engines, instead of using bottled gas as recommended by the AVMA. The Humane Society of Utah criticized the city of Enoch for using exhaust fumes from a pickup truck to kill stray dogs and cats. The Enoch City Council voted unanimously on April 17, [2002] to continue the practice. "Our council says it works; it's the best method and we're not going to cave in" to animal rights groups, City Manager Gaylen Matheson said in a telephone interview. "In forty-five seconds they are sound asleep and in another couple of minutes they are dead," said Matheson, acknowledging "there is a perception problem having a truck do it."

Five years ago Enoch was gassing 450 animals a year. The recent controversy and attendant news stories resulted in an animal welfare group taking many of the animals. There also has been a decline in strays, apparently because pet guardians are being more responsible, Matheson said. The only animals being gassed in Enoch now are dogs that have attacked sheep or otherwise demonstrated viciousness—about three dogs a month. There is no way Enoch's sole part-time animal control officer could use intravenous injection on vicious animals, he said. "It is so unsafe to one person to give the shot," Matheson said. "To all by yourself hold a sheep-killer dog around the neck and try to get that thing in a vein. You just can't do it." [1]

Best Friends Animal Sanctuary has worked with the Enoch shelter as part of "No More Homeless Pets" in Utah. Through making spay/neuter available to that community and with another shelter taking animals from Enoch, the shelter's euthanasia figures have dropped dramatically and they now average around one dog a month. [2]

The American Veterinary Medical Association (AVMA) and the Humane Society of the United States (HSUS) agree that gas chambers should not be overcrowded. In fact, according to the 2000 Report by the AVMA Panel on Euthanasia—*the veterinary medical authority on euthanasia*—"the CO chamber must be of the highest-quality construction and should allow for separation of individual animals." [3]

Another condition of the AVMA panel on carbon monoxide killing is that "the chamber must be well-lit and have view ports that allow personnel direct observation of animals." [4] In contrast, many gas chambers are dark, windowless boxes.

According to the Humane Society of the United States, "Carbon monoxide is a hazardous substance considered especially dangerous because it is odorless, tasteless, colorless, and explosive. Repeated exposure to CO, even at low levels, can result in many serious long-term effects including (but not limited to) cancer, infertility, and heart disease." [5]

Old, young, and sick animals are particularly susceptible to gas-related trauma, since they breathe and circulate oxygen and carbon monoxide differently from healthy adult animals, causing a resistance to hypoxia (oxygen deficiency). For these animals, death by carbon monoxide poisoning is slow and highly stressful and therefore unacceptable. [6]

Death by injection is much faster than gassing. According to the HSUS and the American Humane Association's (AHA) Operational Guide for Animal Care and Control Agencies, *gassing takes at least thirty minutes. This does not include the time needed for emptying the chamber of gas, removing the dead bodies, checking the vital signs of each to ensure the animals really are dead, disposing of the bodies, and cleaning the chamber. Lethal injection, on the other hand, brings about death within two to three minutes.* [7]

Contrary to what some organizations believe, using lethal injection is actually cheaper than gassing. A Western Pennsylvania Humane Society study in 2000 arrived at the conclusion that the cost of gassing 10,000 animals a year averages $13,230, while the cost of lethal injection is $12,700. The cost of gassing is even higher when the additional expense of providing backup lethal injections is factored in. [8]

Lethal injection is more humane, cheaper, and faster. Yet still we use the gas chamber.

"Oh, my God!"

Rosemary Ficken's facial expression says it all. She is either witnessing an act of God or she has completely lost her mind. Grabbing the handle of the trolley, she pulls the blue compartment out of the chamber to get a better look at what she thinks must be a mirage.

Cain is standing atop the mound of dead dogs. His heavy brown eyes fixate on Ficken. His gait is a bit wobbly, but his tail wags—not from happiness but from triumph. He snarls at her.

Ficken is in a state of shock. Never in her fifteen years has any dog or cat survived and cheated death. She wonders if she should re-gas the stubborn canine, but she quickly recants that thought. Ficken grabs the pole noose and laces it around

Rosemary Ficken, who has the heartbreaking task of operating the chamber, loving on a stray.

Photo by Donna Lochmann.

Cain's neck. With shaking hands and disbelief, she walks him to another cage and rushes to make a phone call to me.

Cain is now in Auxiliary, the area just to the side of the gas chamber. Auxiliary is where they put the misfits—the sick, the old, any dog unfortunate enough to have been born a pit bull. This section of the pound isn't full of much hope. Cain peers out of his cage, still standing and watching every move around him. He isn't going to let his guard down, especially now that he knows what it is that they do with you. He seems determined to live.

While I'm sitting at my computer going through my daily lists of e-mails, the phone rings. Since founding Stray Rescue of St. Louis several years ago, I never have received a phone call such as this one—one that turns an incredibly tragic situation into front-page news across the country.

"Please take him. I don't have the heart to put him back in there and re-gas him," Ficken says to me. "I just can't do it, and he really wants to live."

"Don't even think about putting him back in there; of course we will take him," I respond in shock and concern. "How is he? Is he sick or mean or anything?"

"He is mouthy and can be aggressive, but I am looking at him right now and he's wagging his tail," she replies.

"Has this ever happened before?" I ask.

"In all my years I've never seen anything like it." After trying to think of what the hell could have happened, we can only conclude that some type of divine intervention occurred. With that, Ficken hangs up the phone.

If I am to take Cain, his old name has to go. All Stray Rescue dogs get a fresh start, including a new name that carries no baggage. I immediately re-name the survivor "Quentin," after the notorious San Quentin prison, home to California's gas chamber and death row.

I pace in the office, staring at my own pack of once-rejected dogs. Both of Stray Rescue's shelters are full, so I decide to write a news release:

FOR IMMEDIATE RELEASE
DATE: August 6th, 2003
CONTACT: Randy Grim, 314-771-6121

A First for Animal Control—Dog Survives Gas Chamber While Being Destroyed at the City Pound. He Is Now Safe and Getting a Second Chance at Life at Stray Rescue of St. Louis

(St. Louis, MO) Quentin, the male red Basenji mix, didn't want to die yesterday. Animal Control on Gasconade was euthanizing its daily lot of animals. Quentin was in the gas chamber and, after the process was over, lay very much alive amongst the other, dead dogs. "I have never seen anything like this," says Rosemary Ficken of Animal Control. "I just couldn't do it to him again, he really wants to live."

Stray Rescue steps in and makes her wishes a reality.

"He isn't going to die, but live and get a home one day," says Randy Grim of Stray Rescue. "We all agree, if ever there was a dog who deserves a second chance, it is Quentin."

The guests all agree the story is miraculous. They leave feeling compelled to do more to make this world a better, safer place for animals. They leave yearning to go home and hug their companion animals. The dinner party was a success. It is time for me to hug my own pack.

PART TWO

FOUR

Media Frenzy

STRAY RESCUE IS ALWAYS FULL. WITH AN ENDLESS LIST of dogs subsisting on the streets awaiting salvation, extra space is rare. Quentin needs to move out and find a home. The press release is simple: *"Dog Survives Gas Chamber, Now Needs a Home."* I've sent the release via the shelter's antiquated fax machine. Jenn and I are optimistic that at least someone from the media will show up so that Quentin can find his forever home. I head out from my house to pick him up.

I am often asked how I started Stray Rescue of St. Louis. I ask myself that, too. I never devised a game plan or had a vision; I guess it was born out of necessity. I hated my job as a flight attendant. I figured there had to be more to life than saying, "Chicken or beef?" Little did I know that this career move would one day evolve into two no-kill shelters with a legion of 200 volunteers and have an impact on the stray dog crisis in America. I love the dogs I save. I feel their pain, so I keep up the act of "Dog Man" or, as a homeless man calls me, "Coyote Man," so those canines don't suffer and die. That's pretty much why I became the founder of Stray Rescue.

I suffer from social anxiety. I have some phobias. I am gay. I am a shy, private kind of guy—by no means a hero. I have been thrust into the dog limelight from a previous book about my work. It forces me to try to be more outgoing and confident—you know, exude that Rambo-type of confidence.

In 1990 I learned the fine art of cutting dog hair. It's not something I really wanted to do, but I thought it would at least point me in the direction of my dream of working with animals. I'd see stray dogs—some in packs—pass by the Lafayette Square grooming shop where I worked. In an effort to get them off the streets, I'd make the normal calls to the local shelters and government agencies, only to find out that these dogs simply are out of luck. I started to think of ways to catch them, and before long I invented some wacky capture methods. I also enlisted friends to help save these poor creatures. Each year, this makeshift organization grew as I overloaded everyone I knew with a stray dog. Stray Rescue officially was born in 1998 as a full-fledged nonprofit organization and shelter. I still have no idea how I did it, except that I had no choice.

Stray Rescue has received numerous accolades from the American Red Cross and also has received national media attention from Animal Planet, National Geographic, the Weather Channel and Forbes *magazine. Now with Quentin on board, his story has been featured in* People *magazine and on* It's a Miracle *television show.*

In the National Geographic feature, Maryann Mott wrote:

In St. Louis, Randy Grim, founder of Stray Rescue, is out on the streets every day feeding 50 or more mutts.

If these wild dogs don't die of sheer starvation, he said, diseases such as parvovirus, heartworm, or intestinal parasites usually kill them. Their average life span is one to two years.

Many of the animals he sees were once "bait dogs"—smaller, passive animals used to train fighting dogs. Great Dane puppies are commonly used, he said, and wire is twisted around their legs to hold them down, so they can't run while being mauled during training sessions.

"If they live, they are just discarded onto the streets," said Grim. The animals are recognizable by their missing limbs, and scars from the brutal attacks.[1]

Since starting in 1991, I am credited with saving 5,000 feral dogs, all of whom—through months of gentle, loving care—have been turned into house pets and adopted by new families. Some have even gone on to become therapy animals, bringing joy to people in hospitals and nursing homes.

Animal Planet's Wild Rescues *television show featured Stray Rescue in action, saving dogs and cats from abuse and neglect from a dilapidated abandoned puppy mill in Cuba, Missouri. More than seventeen lives were saved, but the woman responsible never was prosecuted.*

Since 1998, more than forty-five households have participated in the Stray Rescue foster family network. These generous people take in sickly, traumatized animals and, with time and the support of professional animal trainers and behaviorists, give back healthy, loving companions ready for adoption. Stray Rescue's foster network is the largest and most effective program of its kind in the St. Louis area. Stray Rescue has made a significant impact and become a voice for stray animals everywhere. With fabulous volunteers, veterinarians, trainers, behaviorists, shelters and programs, I continue to be amazed at how this organization has evolved.

But there is so much more work to do because these poor animals continue to suffer. Some days it feels as if I'm fighting a never-ending battle, but it's a battle that I must wage—for their sake.

On Manchester Road, the shelter flag is visible above a nest of news vans stationed outside the shelter building. As I pull to the side of the building, antennas pierce the sky; television crews prepare for live feeds.

For the love of God, what is going on? Who died or what burned? Surely I would know if something awful had happened. My heart races. Either there has been a disaster or Ed McMahon is here with a million-dollar check. I pop an antacid and sneak into the back entrance of the shelter.

The room is full to bursting with a press corps clutching their microphones, blinding me with their lights and cameras. Knee-high, at the end of this tunnel of

Photo by Donna Lochmann.

Quentin during his stay at Stray Rescue.

confusion, I see a cocked, worried brown face. Our eyes lock. His head floats above stick legs, a skeletal frame and a tucked tail. His eyes could melt, and forever haunt, even the most hardhearted soul. It is evident the dog is still traumatized, and now he has to endure this.

Quentin looks bewildered. So do I, and I think I cock my head too.

They are here for Quentin.

I whisper to myself, "Oh, God help me." Quentin is thinking the dog version of "Oh, God help me."

I career into anxious media mode. They fire questions. The dogs in the shelter bark, loud and furiously.

"How many dogs were in the gas chamber with him?"

"Are there any side effects from the chamber?"

A cameraman runs a microphone up my shirt.

I explain Quentin's plight and the death of the seven dogs he stood upon, tell them how he got his name, give a minute-by-minute account of the rescue. All the while, I just want to nurture the "miracle dog." I want to hold his small body, to let him know he's found a safe place. It won't be an intimate moment. I push my way through the media toward the office door to greet my new four-legged friend, the wonder dog, even though the questions keep coming.

Cameras circle like vultures while I slowly kneel down to get a good look at the dog, and give him a good look at me. I reach for him with my hand, and he gives it a slow, deliberate kiss. Fear of cameras and reporters evaporates. It's just Quentin and me.

"Your bad days are behind you, buddy. You're in good hands now," I whisper as I stroke the smooth, round top of his head, between his radar-like ears that are finally up, eyes squinting in ecstasy from this simple act of compassion. I can't help but think in his short lifespan that this is a rare event for this dog whom the people at the pound called "mouthy and aggressive."

Quentin accepts Milk Bones from anyone who offers one and begins to relax. It is obvious that his mind is processing all this new information and a conclusion is about to register: *This beats the hell out of the city pound.*

While photographers grab the first shots of Quentin, I am pulled away to do an interview with the Associated Press. We cover the same questions and answers from before, and naively, I think it's business as usual. I have no idea that Associated Press stands for "you will have no sleep for a solid week." It is the wire service to all national media, the backbone and central nervous system of America's news.

After the white vans pull away, calm is restored at the shelter. Only then do I notice the horrible but all-too-familiar cough. Within minutes Quentin visits the veterinarian next door. I go home to regroup and digest what has just happened.

There is no digesting. The Associated Press already has worked its magic. CNN is airing clips every thirty minutes and every local television and radio station is running the story of a dog who is quickly becoming "as famous as Rin Tin Tin."

The calls won't stop. From the public, from the media, from my mom. Every media outlet I can think of wants a piece of Quentin, which means a piece of me, too. I crave a martini or some liquid form of escaping. My initial reaction to any attention is to run away, but I have to be the rescue professional and face the music. I have pills for this. It is time to take one and meet this frenzy head-on.

Getting a home for Quentin has, at breakneck speed, evolved into "How do we turn this attention for a freak of nature or novelty piece into a sober look at gas chambers in the United States?" I have to think fast and on my feet.

"Randy, is it OK for Fox News to do a live feed for its five o'clock show?"

"Hey, Randy, *People* magazine needs to talk to you. They will be here in the morning."

"Oh, Randy, the *Today Show* called, and here is a list of ten others and we are getting applications for Quentin by the hundreds." Jenn's play-by-play media updates only cause more anxiety.

The *Today Show*?

Think *Close Encounters*. That's my backyard at 3 a.m. Every conceivable kind of light is trained on the spot where Quentin and I will stand in a few hours when we are telling his story to the entire continent via *The Today Show*. I am shaking. Quentin is sleeping. I haven't slept since meeting my new-found miracle. Fearless Jenn, Stray Rescue's only employee, sits in my kitchen. Like two kids playing hide and seek, we look out the windows of my three-story Victorian home and howl at the movie set in my backyard.

"Jenn, I can't do this. . . . Do I look fat?" I'm trying to joke. Jenn laughs.

A perky woman with a clipboard ascends the stairs around 5 a.m.

"Hi! I'm the producer of the segment. We will need you in forty-five minutes. Don't worry, there will only be 5.4 million viewers today because it's Saturday!"

She keeps on talking, but I don't hear another word.

Oblivious, Quentin has arisen, running around the kitchen, playing hard. He has it easy—he just has to sit there and look cute for the cameras. I want to be the dog. His kennel cough is still very noticeable, but other than the cough, he behaves as if he has lived with me from the day he was born. If there are any side effects from the gas chamber, I can't tell. I am living with the Harry Houdini of the dog world.

It's show time. Quentin and I take our marks. Quentin's fine. Beads of sweat form on my upper lip. Here's an excerpt from our appearance:

The Today Show:

NATALIE MORALES, co-host: Every dog has its day, and for one dog, that day came at just the right time. Quentin, a one-year-old mixed breed, cheated death when he managed to survive a city pound gas chamber. And joining Quentin to tell us about this small miracle is Randy Grim, founder of Stray Rescue of St. Louis.

Good morning, Randy. Good morning, Quentin. He's looking good today.

RANDY GRIM: Good morning.

MORALES: So great to see you.

GRIM: Fantastic. Oh, thank you.

MORALES: Tell us what exactly happened with Quentin and—and how did you find him?

GRIM: Sure. I'm the founder of Stray Rescue of St. Louis, and we do work with the city pound and try—we save the dogs who are either injured or shot, or the ones that are going to the gas chamber. So I got a call from the supervisor at the pound, and she said, "Randy, you're not going to believe this." And I go, "What?" And she said, "I gassed our normal lot of dogs, and when I opened the door, standing on top of the dead dogs was Quentin." Staring at her in the face, wagging his tail.

MORALES: It's truly remarkable, Randy.

GRIM: And she—yeah. And she said—I said, "Has this ever happened before?" And she—she said, "Absolutely never. Never since we've had the gas chamber."

And—and then she said, "I don't have the heart to gas him." I said, "Oh, no, don't. I'm on my way, I'll take him."

MORALES: So what condition was he in when you saw him?

GRIM: You know, I keep saying that he's—you know, besides the miracle, I keep calling him the messiah of dogs. I keep waiting to see him turn Milk Bones into wine. Because he—he actually looked fantastic. He has a little bit of kennel cough right now, but he is wonderful, and I—I'm really enjoying keeping him here at my house.

MORALES: Why the name Quentin? Where did you come up with that?

GRIM: It's after the prison, San Quentin. I feel like Quentin, this Quentin, beat all odds, escaped from prison and cheated death. And I really feel like he's here to tell a message and to give a message about, you know, first of all, about how horrible the gas chamber is. We don't use it on people anymore. So, I hear Quentin speaking. . . .[2]

Little did I know how loud Quentin's voice was destined to become.

The crew packs up and leaves while Quentin and I lie down for an hour. He sleeps in my arms while I lie awake just looking at him, trying to answer the questions myself, the questions I have been asked over and over again. I still don't have any real answers, but I know by the way he nestles his furry muzzle under my chin that Quentin is content. The bliss is short-lived, for *People* magazine is next and is scheduled to arrive any minute.

They do. Kate Klise, an attractive reporter who oozes kindness, is easy to talk to. Quentin seems to like her, as well. She is compassionate, so the interview is easy enough. Having been awake for more than twenty-four hours, I need an easy interview and after all the excitement so does Quentin. But "if it seems too good to be true, then it usually is." *People*'s photographer shows up and the word "easy" doesn't exist anymore. I watch the word "sleep" follow "easy" into oblivion.

The minutes pass like molasses dripping from a stick as Quentin and I strike many different poses. Hours pass. Sleep-deprived, I just want the nice man with the camera to catch his flight home. But he has bigger plans for us—a walk in the park.

"No."

It has been eight hours of shooting already, and thirty-two hours since I have seen a bed. Quentin is getting perturbed as well. For both our sakes, I blurt out, "Quentin has had enough too—let's hurry this up." Maybe the photographer will feel more sympathy for Quentin than he does for this sleep-deprived rescue robot. He takes the bait and it is over.

Why has one little dog who survived received all this attention, when millions of dogs are destroyed in the U.S. each year?

Joseph Spohn, a producer for NBC's Today Show *and* 60 Minutes, *says, "I think America is fascinated with animal stories, especially stories about our domesticated pets, because we are a nation that likes to think we love the less fortunate. Having beaten down nature, tamed the frontier, as well as the British Empire and every other nation on earth, we relish helping the critters beneath us. Where would they be without us? Eaten, no doubt. If it weren't for our towering position on the food chain, our big brains and mechanical brawn—cats, dogs—the lot of them, would all be up against more savage competitors. Still, we know deep down they have what we lose sight of too often—a direct connection to the here and now, an awareness of the most important things in life—affection, trust, loyalty, playfulness, and true, cosmic love."* [3]

Sarah Casey Newman, a columnist for the St. Louis Post Dispatch, *offers, "I can think of plenty of reasons why America loves animal stories—and especially one like Quentin's, since his really is one of those rare, against-all-odds miracles that people need to hear about to give their faith a boost and provide a little light of hope in a rather dark world. People get tired of hearing all the bad news that's out there. They really ache for the warm fuzzy stories—and what's warmer or fuzzier than an animal story, especially one about an animal who was so determined to live, no mat - ter how lousy his life, that he survived a gas chamber? To me, the sad thing is that there are so many wonderful animal stories out there that don't see the light of day because they don't have the 'news' value that Quentin's story does."* [4]

The guest bedroom is spacious, housing a queen-size bed with a down comforter. Since Quentin still has kennel cough it's best to keep him separate from my own clan. We both dive into the cozy bed and what happens next is truly a miracle. We sleep. Quentin experiences a real bed and someone to hold and love him. But I already have five "misfits," and Hannah could make his life miserable. I can't keep him.

FIVE

He Is All Mine

QUENTIN MAKES HIMSELF AT HOME IN ONE OF THE accommodating dog apartments back at Stray Rescue's safe haven. Although the thought of putting him back behind bars bothers me, I have no choice. I can't keep him, even though I really want to keep him, or at least to foster him.

My fostering days have been very limited since my pit bull-mix "kid," Hannah, was rescued five years ago. To put it bluntly, Hannah is a bully and known as the "Queen Bitch" of the house. She loathes all other dogs except for the pack she lives with—and that took years of training and praying to the dog gods for help. Hannah showed little mercy to the dogs I did foster. A garden hose for fight prevention and separate bedrooms for the strays were my only trustworthy safeguards. With so many applications for Quentin's adoption coming at high speed, it just wouldn't be fair for me to keep him. I keep telling myself this. *Anyway, I should be able to place him easily.* God knows, there will be another dog in need that I will have to take in.

Quentin's new view isn't of a gas chamber or of dead dogs being thrown into the back of a truck anymore, but of cheery pictures and an endless supply of treats and toys. His life now consists of special walks, playing in the yard, food, toys, and most importantly, lots of love from the volunteers. Because of his newfound fame, Quentin is getting plenty of doting from everyone—and I mean *everyone.* He is digging it. I see a very spoiled little Basenji mix in our future.

A half-off sale at Bloomingdale's couldn't have attracted more attention to our shelter. The only thing missing, as a nonstop stream of well-wishers and potential adopters enters the shelter, is a revolving door. This is a welcome sight, I think. Every dog at the shelter will be adopted and that will be my own miniature marvel.

It doesn't happen. Quentin takes the spotlight away from the other just-as-deserving stray dogs who also need forever homes. I envision the rest of the strays plotting how to get Quentin out and increase their own chances at adoption.

Armani, the purebred Akita two pens down from the pin-up pooch, must be

41

livid. He too came from the pound. He too was destined to die, and he too has suffered. Armani was brought into the city pound by the police with a deadly thirty-pound chain embedded into his neck. Emergency surgeries saved his life but nobody knew his story. He wasn't famous, and even as I sit here and type this in 2004, Armani is still waiting at the shelter for his big day. The day he finally goes home.

The applications for Quentin now exceed 700, including one from as far away as Japan and one from a family that lives in San Quentin. Elated to see the outpouring of concern and want, I know I had better start interviewing potential adopters—and without delay, before the nasty calls start. Impatient calls and e-mails are already clogging our phone system like cholesterol in hardening arteries.

"Why are they not applying for any of the others?" I ask Jenn.

"I guess everyone wants a famous dog," she replies, knowing I am about to snap.

"Then I want to slap everyone—they don't get it," I say. "Don't people understand the real story is the mound of dogs who died, that he was standing on top of? If all 700 people went out and adopted just one dog from their shelters, then those dogs didn't die in vain. And what is up with people in Japan and London wanting him, are they nuts—for the love of God?"

Still pissed, I continue. "Let's just lie and paint every damn dog orange and say they are Quentin." I am cursing like a sailor, frustrated that the adoption rate isn't increasing.

With only Jenn available to handle the onslaught of keyed-up calls, I recruit volunteers to help staff the phones. It's really insane; the calls keep coming—and so do the media. It's impossible to escape. I wonder if Quent understands the pandemonium he has unleashed. Craving some type of normalcy, I grab a stack of applications and sneak out to head home, as does Jenn.

That evening, my phone rings repeatedly. I turn the maddening ringer off. If I let them go to Call Notes, it will be easier to simply listen to the draining messages in one sweeping blow. I crawl into my bed, and with a pad, a pen, a stack of applications, and four dogs, I go fetal for a while.

It's getting late, but with dread I decide to listen to the messages.

Beep: "Hi I got your number from a friend and I really want to adopt Quentin. He will have a great home. My name is . . . "

I can't believe it—one of the wealthiest families in St. Louis wants to adopt him. Surely they would be a good home! I toss the cluster of applications on the nightstand and reach for the phone.

"Hi. This is Randy with Stray Rescue and I am calling about your interest in Quentin."

A home visit is set for tomorrow, and I think I have a home for him. Not even listening to the rest of the calls, I roll over, put my arm around Hannah and fall asleep with a grin.

Excited to tell her the good news, I meet Jenn at a local diner the first thing in the morning.

"Quentin may be going to a home, and not just any home," I say. I tell her the name.

"You've got to be kidding me," she exclaims.

"Will you go with me to his home?" I know she will say yes. Stray Rescue can only provide Jenn and me with the wherewithal for the most basic lifestyles. Dog aside, we are both curious about how the other half lives.

We head to the shelter to pick up Quentin. Jenn starts telling me about some of the more bizarre applications. There are many, ranging from "I must have him for it is a sign from God that I do," to ones from people holding impressive jobs such as that of a national news anchor. We both laugh a lot during the drive, feeling as if we are holding Lassie hostage.

Quentin is delighted to see me. As I get him out of his pen at the shelter, he plants a deliberate kiss on my cheek. The consummate professional, I try hard not to make too much eye contact with him. I have to love them all—no favorites—though he is absolutely adorable and working hard to make me cave in.

In the car Quentin sits just like a passenger on a Sunday drive, looking out the window. Jenn and I feed him many treats and talk for the twentieth time about what it must have been like for him at the city pound. As we pull into the trendy neighborhood, knowing we are probably inching closer to his forever home, I reach around and pet his muzzle. Before us stands a beautiful, turn-of-the-century Victorian house.

A happy and playful yellow Labrador retriever and his guardian, a young man, greet us at the pearly gates. The perfectly manicured yard is large by city standards, and at first glance it looks like a home in which I would place any dog. We all take a seat on the deck and watch as Quentin and the Lab begin to play, dashing up and down the privacy fence line. It looks very promising.

"You have a beautiful dog there," I say.

"Yeah, he is a pretty good dog. I like to take him to my country house. He is a good boy and goes with me hunting too."

The word "hunting" bothers me, but I also know that it doesn't mean it is a bad home. I just wish people thought like I do: God made grocery stores so we don't have to run around with guns and shoot animals. I try to ignore the hunting comment and instead try to peek at the Lab's backside. Each time he sprints by, I twist my neck to see if he had his, well, balls.

"If you trying to see if he's neutered, yes, he is, and he sleeps in bed with me, too." I flush red from the collar of my shirt to my hairline knowing he caught me eyeing his dog's privates.

"If you can't have Quentin, would you be interested in another dog?" Jenn asks. There is an awkward silence, which is broken when the homeowner asks us if we would like something to drink.

Watching Quentin run and play is a real treat, and the potential new guardian is certainly nice enough. He even has a special enclosure where the Lab can hang out in the yard or go through a small maze into the main house. Both dogs really seem to be getting along. But something is bothering me about the whole possible adoption. As we leave, Jenn and I each receive a departing gift of fresh homegrown tomatoes and head toward the car.

"I promise to get back to you very soon and thanks for being so nice," I say.

In the car, the scrutiny begins.

"What bothered you about this home visit?" I ask Jenn, wondering if we are thinking alike.

"He only wants Quentin?" she quizzes.

"*Bingo*. I mean, he's nice and I love his dog, but . . ."

As we arrive at my house, Paul Schankman of the local Fox News affiliate awaits us.

"Hey Randy, can we talk a little bit? Does Quentin have a home yet?" he asks.

"He might. We still have a lot of applications to go through," I say.

Schankman then asks if he can follow his progress for a couple months for a bigger story in November. I don't mind at all. Paul has become my favorite reporter to work with and does really great news pieces. The news van departs and Quentin now gets to run and play in my ungroomed backyard—quite a change from the place we just came from.

As Jenn and I watch Quentin play in the yard, I am more confused than ever about how to adopt out Quent. If I can't even adopt him to the wealthiest family in St. Louis, how will I find him a home that will love him for just being himself, a dog, and a companion? When his fifteen minutes of fame are up, he will be just another dog capable of pooping in the house, eating furniture, and knocking over trash cans.

I walk up my back stairs to get some food for Quentin and, accidentally, my pack of four charges out the door. My heart pounds and I scream, "Hannah hates other dogs—she'll *kill* him!"

"Jenn, grab the hose," I holler as I accelerate down the stairs to tackle Hannah.

"Oh, Randy, hurry!" Jenn yells.

It's too late. Hannah, my seventy-five-pound pit bull mix, is eye to eye with Quentin. First contact.

What happens next is another canine miracle. Hannah falls to the ground and rolls over into a passive position. She then stands up and repeatedly licks Quentin's muzzle.

I now hold the hose in my trembling hands. "This can't be happening," I whisper to Jenn, thinking that if I speak any louder a fight will ensue.

Hannah and Quentin then start to play a game of doggy tag. They wrestle and play some more, and then both walk up to me with their tails wagging. I think I hear them say, *See, Dad, we love each other.* This is not the tyrant Hannah I've known for five years. I always call her my macho girl; beating up other dogs seemed bred into her. Did Quentin really perform a miracle on her? Is he the messiah of dogs?

Photo by Donna Lochmann.

Can he stay, Dad? Please?

"Well, there's no need for him to go back to the shelter," I say. "He can stay here until we find his forever home. Anyway, he was just hurting the chances for the other dogs to get a home."

Jenn agrees, grinning from ear to ear. Hannah gives Quentin a kiss.

Quentin and Hannah sit at my feet as I listen to my new messages in my office. One message really catches my attention. It is from Dr. Elliot Katz of In Defense of Animals (IDA), a national animal protection organization.

He wants to sponsor a national campaign, with Quentin as the poster child. The money raised will pay for a veterinarian and injections so we can rid our city of the barbaric gas chamber. I think I hear angels sing as I listen to his message.

It becomes apparent what I have to do next. Finding Quentin the right home is obvious to me now. It is right under my nose—or should I say my feet. He is home. My home. It won't be fair to place him in a home and then pull him out if we have to do awareness appearances. He has a job to do, probably his half of the pact he made

Photo by Donna Lochmann.

Quentin and Hannah hanging out with Dad on the bed.

with the doggy god in the gas chamber. Quentin can make a difference by teaming up with me so we can save many more animals from the fate that he avoided.

I realize that once I announce that I am keeping him, folks may become outraged. I become somewhat afraid. I now envision a scene from the movie *Frankenstein*—an angry mob of 700 people with torches banging on my door! I know in my heart that I am doing the right thing, mob or no mob. I write a news release that again will go nationwide and overseas—and once again fuel the media frenzy.

Photo by Jenn Foster.

Quentin and Dad.

FOR IMMEDIATE RELEASE
Aug. 12, 2003

Press conference and benefit is:
DATE: Aug. 15, 2003
TIME: 6-8 p.m.
PLACE: Stray Rescue's Manchester Shelter, 5321 Manchester Road
CONTACT: Randy Grim, 314-771-6121

THE GAS CHAMBER-SURVIVING DOG, QUENTIN, GOES TO HIS NEW HOME. FUNDING TO RID CHAMBER BEGINS; THE CELEBRATION BENEFIT IS THIS FRIDAY.
THE MIRACLE CONTINUES!

(St. Louis) Quentin, the miracle dog who is the first dog to survive the city's gas chamber, goes to his forever home with Randy Grim, founder of Stray Rescue of St. Louis. In Defense of Animals has stepped up with $5,000, earmarking this amount toward ridding St. Louis of its gas chamber as its primary euthanasia method and affording a veterinarian. The press conference and benefit will be this Friday at 6 p.m. at 5321 Manchester, a Stray Rescue shelter.

"Not only do I love him and my other dogs love Quentin, but he lived to serve a higher purpose. Living with me, he can continue to educate the public and help the millions of animals who do not make it out of America's shelters alive," says Grim. "I am his guardian."

IDA contacted Grim yesterday with the news about the funding and Quentin becoming the poster child for a new national campaign to bring awareness to the plight of all shelter and homeless animals who die, and bring to light the horror of puppy mills, and the breeding, buying, and selling of animals.

The benefit will have Quentin there to meet his well-wishers. Grim will be on hand to sign copies of his critically acclaimed book, *The Man Who Talks to Dogs* (St. Martin's Press). There also will be food, items for sale and, most importantly, dogs for adoption. All proceeds benefit Stray Rescue and the Animal House Fund, a fund for a new animal control facility. Quentin will be featured in this Friday's *People* magazine.

"Stray Rescue wants to thank the 700 people who wanted to adopt Quentin and encourage them to adopt a dog, famous or not. And for the record, Quentin will not only be educating children, adults and the nation, but also sleeping in bed, eating great food, and playing with toys and new brothers and sisters, knowing that his bad days are behind him for good," Grim says.

SIX

A Star Is Born

TELEVISION PRODUCERS ARE CALLING. FROM *RIPLEY'S Believe It or Not* to NBC's *The John Walsh Show,* they all want Quentin. The *Sharon Osborne Show* wants exclusive rights to his story. It's getting crazy and, though I know his story needs to be told, what shows do we choose? Which best serves the larger story? We agree, it's John Walsh.

"Randy, can Quentin travel in the cargo bin of a plane?" asks the producer.

"Oh, my God, *NO!* There is no way I would ever put any of my 'kids' in the cargo bin," I reply. "Cargoes aren't safe for animals. Isn't there something else you can do?"

Exasperated: "We will get back to you."

Quentin lies by my feet as I hang up the phone. He gives me his Love Look—butter would melt—and I know I did the right thing. I sit at my desk thinking of ways to get my own agenda on the show, the plight of the strays—the eighty-million-plus on the streets—and how to rid the country of the gas chamber. Not something most Americans want to hear about during the chat hour.

The word "miracle" has been used so often to describe Quentin. To me, the greater miracle is that we are together in the same city, the same house and the same family. Our bond was quick and real.

The producer calls back with travel arrangements. Quentin can ride in the cabin of the plane. I jump up out my chair with a silent *Hooray!* Then it hits me: he may have no manners on a plane, or worse. Much worse. I see Quent freaking out, attacking the flight crew, maiming passengers. I see the *Ripley's* cover: *"Miracle Dog Goes Berserk."* I'm pondering this when all hell breaks loose in the Grim household. Hannah is chasing Miracle Dog up and down the hall—he's got a pillow in his mouth, and it's raining feathers. He doesn't stop when I yell. In fact, for a fleeting moment, he shoots me an evil grin. Did I see an evil grin? I start chasing both of them; this only gets the entire pack in on the game.

"Quentin, you are to set the example," I say.

49

All five stare at me; I see the machinations behind their eyes. I am the no-fun kid in school, the nerd on the playground. In unison, to the nanosecond, they promptly snub my command. I surrender, but not before snatching the pillow. I clutch what's left of it and watch Quentin and his cohorts chase and play, wrestling in a pile of feathers. I am getting on a plane, going on a national TV show with the worst-behaved dog on the planet. I need the miracle . . . or a drink.

Departure is just a few days away. I must make sure Quentin has everything he needs for the trip. I make sure Stray Rescue is in good enough shape to function without me for four days. I review my checklist. Traveling papers for Quent, *check*. Treats, food and bowls, *check*. Suitcase packed with outdated clothes for Dad, *check*. Valium for Quent, *check*. Valium for Dad, *check*.

I am on top of it for a change. Organizational skills are not one of my strengths. I am obsessing over this trip. I worry Quentin may hate it. After all, he's leading a normal life at home, and now I will find out how he handles the limelight and many different types of people. New Yorkers are a tough audience. They'll see Quent and me as so much pap. I already know that, in the spotlight, my own anxiety level goes stratospheric, straight off the charts; I am banking on Quent to pull it off so I can focus on my own anxieties. I say a prayer. That night I don't sleep at all.

Getting out of the house is never easy, especially with just one of the dogs and that huge giveaway—a suitcase. As every dog (or cat) guardian knows, your animals know you are going away before you do. They know it the minute you think about going away. The dogs stare at me, aghast at the sheer treachery of making off with only Quentin. You know the tacky picture of the four dogs playing poker? That would be my clan, scheming to get even. . . . Well, there goes the house and one pissed-off group of dogs. "Act normal," I whisper to Quentin as we tiptoe down the stairs.

Jenn and her husband Darrell taxi Quentin and me to the airport. I ricochet between excitement and high anxiety. Quentin sits on my lap staring out the window; every few minutes, he turns around to give me a kiss. In return, I repeat over and over, "Make Daddy proud," realizing I make a horrible stage mother.

We pull up to Lambert Field's curbside check-in—and a camera crew from Fox 2 News. Quent wags his tail. Two weeks ago, nobody on this earth gave a damn about this beyond-lovable little guy. Now his arrival at the airport merits Fox News coverage.

"Mr. Grim, here is your ticket," says the skycap. "I need to see I.D. for Quentin Grim." The skycap looks in Darrell's direction. I point my finger toward the wagging pooch with the perky ears.

"Oh. Well, here is your first-class ticket, Mr. Quentin," says the skycap, and we all laugh.

"Isn't he the dog who lived through being gassed?" he asks.

"That would be him," I reply.

"Wow, talk about rags to riches. Even I haven't flown first class," the skycap says as he grabs our luggage. Then he pets Quentin in a manner that shows real compassion. I thought to myself, *Quent touched his heart. That is so cool.* The camera follows us as we walk inside the airport. Soon, there is a crowd.

My own anxiety peaks as passengers and airport employees take turns to get a picture with the star pooch. I feel beads of sweat on my upper lip, a sweat 'stache. I know I am beet red. I want to run back to the car; however, I remain and watch in amazement as Quentin turns on the charm and plays the part of a celebrity perfectly.

Getting through security quickly at an airport is difficult, and traveling with Quent makes the task more daunting. We activate every alarm the security station has. Quentin is swiped by the magic wand, then I am told to take off my shoes and perform calisthenics while being swiped by the security officer's probing wand. Onlookers snap pictures. I feel like fainting. Before we leave security, we pose with the entire security staff for a picture, holding up the line. I reach for a Xanax.

Finally free, we're edging our way through the crowded C concourse when an American Airlines representative approaches us. She has a clipboard.

"I see we have a celebrity dog traveling with us. Mr.Grim, has everything been smooth thus far and is there anything I can do to help?"

We continue walking to the gate with the nice lady and I blurt out, "Please, just get us on the plane fast . . . too many people and so many pictures."

She looks at me like I'm crazy, so I explain to her that I suffer from social anxiety and I am a bit freaked out by everything.

"You should be more like your dog," she says.

"If only." I give her a shaky smile.

Quentin hops right into his seat and glances out the window. The entire crew comes to greet us. They take more pictures.

"Would you both care for a drink before we take off?" asks the flight attendant.

That's music to my ears. "Oh yes. I'll have a Bloody Mary and Quent will have water please."

She brings the drinks and I laugh—Quent is being served Evian bottled water.

"Quent, don't expect bottled water at home," I whisper into his rabbit ears.

Quentin enjoying the high society life of flying first class on American Airlines.

The passengers begin to board, and each one walks by the nervous man and his dog. Many stop to chat and pet my baby. I know dogs well, and I'm truly amazed at Quent's behavior. How in the heck does he know when to be Quentin the Star instead of Quentin the Hyperactive Goofy Troublemaker?

Jet engines roar and we're off, destination New York. Quent looks out the window, and behaves like any human passenger with a window seat. He cocks his head to the left, then to the right as the houses and cars below grow smaller. The little motor in his canine brain is working overtime as he takes it all in. His ability to absorb what is going on around him and to register a sane reaction is uncanny. Unlike his Dad.

"Today you have a choice of the chicken or the shrimp salad."

"I will have the salad, and Quentin will have the chicken." I can't believe I'm ordering dinner on a plane for a dog. I smile.

His chicken is served on fine china, accompanied by linens and another glass of Evian. Quent inhales the chicken; without being asked, the flight attendants bring another plate. He polishes off his second course, and then does what any former unwanted dog would do—he begs. I marvel at another of his many talents. He works the entire first-class section, moving from row to row. His moves: a tight, way-cute sit, then he cocks his head, playing up those sad puppy-dog eyes. Quent scores goodies from every passenger. When he's finished, as if on cue, he leaps right back into his seat. The kind flight attendant covers him in a blanket so he can take his nap. We both fall asleep with smiles on our faces.

We arrive at Newark Airport and are greeted by another airline representative, who promptly escorts us to the baggage claim. Once again a crowd surrounds us for a photo op. It dawns on me that Quentin is a national celebrity, and I even sign autographs for him. I guess I work for Quentin now.

The limo driver is holding a sign with both our names. He gathers our luggage and we follow him to . . . This has to be a mistake—he's led us to the longest white stretch limousine I have ever seen. Feeling awkward as hell, I let Quent jump in. Embarrassed, I slink in behind him. We could sure use the money the limo costs to support more dogs at the shelter.

Our traveling chunk of real estate has a bar, multiple televisions, and a stereo system with an intercom so I can communicate with the driver, who seems miles away from us, up front. *This is insane,* I think. Quentin sprints a few laps around the seating area, which can easily accommodate twenty people.

The stretch limo pulls away from the airport with Quentin's little head sticking out the window, sniffing the New Jersey air. I surprise myself and start to cry. Not just a few tears, but almost a sob. With Quent on my lap, I hold him tight with my head resting on his torso and think about how just a few weeks ago he was about to die, unwanted, unloved, skin and bones. And then the image of him in the chamber prompts the floodgates to open. I cry tears of sadness and then of joy, the joy of knowing he will never suffer again. As the skycap in St. Louis said, Quent really has gone from rags to riches. I am so happy for him.

As we cruise the New York City streets, I keep the window cracked so Quentin can keep his head out the window and soak up the sights and scents while I hide behind the tinted part of the glass. It appears as if this giant white limo has only one passenger—a dog. New Yorkers point and laugh as we make our way to the hotel.

The limo pulls up in front of an imposing, historic-looking building on Forty-ninth Street. I have never seen the likes of such a hotel—the W New York. The doorman races to the car.

"Welcome to the W New York, Mr. Grim," he says and smiles as he helps Quentin out of the car. He escorts us to the expanse of the lobby's front desk.

"Mr. Grim, your room is ready, and we have a feather bed waiting for Quentin."

I don't speak. My jaw drops to the floor and I don't even notice the small crowd around Quentin, each vying for their turn with Quent until I hear, "Mr. Grim . . . Mr. Grim?"

Back to reality. I wish I had splurged on new luggage because my outdated brown suitcase with dog bite marks is a bit embarrassing for such a swanky place. We follow the bellman past the art deco bar, and then pass the marble columns to the elevators. Without hesitation, Quent hops into the elevator as if he has done this a thousand times. *How does he know?* Entering the room, my jaw drops again. There is a beautiful feathered dog bed, bowls, toys and—for Dad—the most amazing minibar I have ever seen. *Would it be tacky to steal the dog bed for the shelter dogs? I mean, people do steal soaps and towels, right?*

Quentin blows off the dog bed as if it isn't good enough, and jumps up with his squeaky toy onto one of the two people-beds. I pour a glass of merlot and start making the necessary calls to let friends know the dynamic duo has arrived safely.

We kick back in the bed, watch TV and we—okay, I—ransack the minibar. This is the life. What more can anyone ask for?

The idyll doesn't last long.

Morning arrives too quickly and I wake up virtually percolating with anxiety. It is Show Day. How to calm down? I stare at the minibar, debating a wake-up cocktail. I opt for deep breathing exercises. On my tenth exhale, Quentin sits in front of me with his leash between his teeth. I throw on some sweats and off we go. If you have ever been to New York City with a dog, there is one major problem—no grass, no grass anywhere—just concrete and tall buildings. We walk miles and I could tell my little boy is "holding it," just waiting for a patch of grass. Finally, we frantically set upon three weeds sticking out of a small crack in the sidewalk. Quentin rationalizes, this is as good as it gets. He squats on the weeds. Then it's time to get ready for NBC.

My younger sister, Debbie, a New Yorker and former Golden Gloves heavyweight champion, arrives to tell me how to look "cool." She dresses me in black— I am in New York—and a burnt orange shirt. She hates my hair. Quent needs no primping—lucky dog. I've done Animal Planet segments and dozens of interviews for *The Man Who Talks to Dogs*, but Debbie still lectures both of us for about an hour about television etiquette. We take off to the lobby for yet another limo ride, but now I am afraid and Quentin is overly calm, almost tranquilized. Not a good situation.

"Wow, it looks just like what you see on TV," I say to Debbie as we arrive at the NBC studios. Two NBC employees whisk us from the limo and take us through a back entrance onto a freight elevator. The cage doors of the cargo elevator open and we're taken to dressing room No. 3, our holding area. "Holding" is really right on the mark—we are stuck in the room for the next five hours.

We spend time signing releases, going over questions, and doing hair and makeup—lots of makeup. Now I know why everyone looks so good on television.

"Randy, will Quentin run to you from the back of the studio, down a flight of stairs onto the stage, and into your arms?" asks the producer.

"No idea. He never had to do that before—he isn't Lassie," I reply.

"Let's do a practice run before we let the studio audience in. Follow me."

I see cameras everywhere, a stage, and a miniature stadium of seats. Lights cover the ceiling and sides of the fake studio walls. I have no medication with me, but I would have taken fertilizer to calm my nerves. Quentin, of course, seems fine. The producer takes Quentin, and this is the first time I have ever seen my kid show any signs of panic. Quentin whimpers and stares at me as if saying, *Where are they taking me?* Oh, I don't like this idea already.

Quentin is gone; I am seated on the stage. The producer calls for action, and I stand up and yell, "Come here, Quent, come to Daddy." Quentin appears at the head of the steps, hundreds of feet away. We lock eyes; he sprints down the stairs, heading directly toward me. *What a smart boy I have,* I think, as he gets closer to my outstretched arms. Then I feel a breeze. Quentin passes me like a truck on the turnpike and vanishes through two giant doors. He's on the loose.

The entire crew and I chase him through other television sets. Finally, he stops on a dime and walks up to me as if nothing had happened. *See, Dad, that's what you get for handing me to a stranger.*

"We won't practice that again, but we will still do it at show time even if it takes us a few tries," says the producer.

"Well, whoever takes Quent, can you have them spend some time with him first so he isn't as afraid?" I ask.

"No problem," the producer replies.

Back in the green room, Quentin eats all the cheese and sandwiches as we await our baptism into the world of daytime talk. Debbie, Quent, and I pace the room. There's a knock on the door. The young man Quentin seems to like most takes him away. He's already a professional; this time, he looks back only once. Moments later, there is another knock—I am taken into the studio. By now, I'd like a meal and a nap.

The set is very close to the audience in the first row. My heart is pounding so hard that I can barely swallow. The studio is packed. My knees are shaking.

"We're ready for you, Randy." I take my mark on a plush chair next to John Walsh.

Oh Lord, get me the hell out of here, I think to myself.

The music starts, the applause begins and the questions commence. *Please God let words come out of my mouth! And, please God, get me the HELL out of here!*

The words come out fine, as though someone else has invaded my body. I talk about Stray Rescue with passion. The audience sees pictures of the stray dogs I work with every day. We discuss *The Man Who Talks to Dogs,* and then comes the film clip—the story of Quentin and the media circus the day after his life was spared. Tears are streaming from the eyes of nearly everyone in the audience. So much for hardened New Yorkers.

"Well, Randy, I think it is time for everyone to meet the miracle dog," says John Walsh.

"Ladies and gentlemen, Quentin."

And there he stands, my tan baby who seems very far away. We look at each other, and he sprints down the stairs as the roar of the audience grows louder. He gets nearer and I'm not buying it, but Quentin is smiling as he performs another miracle—he leaps into my arms and plants kisses on my face. Then he hits his mark perfectly and sits right under my feet. John Walsh hands Quent an enormous bone, the size of his thirty-pound frame, and the audience laughs. Quent is ecstatic as he gnaws on the colossal white rawhide. Nothing goes wrong with this dog.

After the show, we do more photos and I sign copies of my book. I am on Cloud Nine, knowing the show went off without a hitch. Deb has tears in her eyes, and we hug backstage. She hugs Quentin, and he gives his Aunt Deb a kiss.

"You want to have a drink, Randy, and celebrate?" she asks.

"Amen, sista."

"Oh, by the way, there's a message for you, from a show called *It's a Miracle.*"

"Let's just go grab a drink," I say. The three of us—a proud Dad, a new Aunt, and one wagging tail—exit the NBC studios.

Photo by Kelly Brinkman.

John Walsh, Quentin, and Randy backstage after the miraculous performance.

Because I am a man of habit, and because Quent can stay with me there at a sidewalk table, while in New York I eat every meal at a restaurant called Café San Martin, around the corner from the hotel. The owners know who Quentin is—hell, most of New York does. Hardened New Yorkers have fallen like bricks for Quentin. This means many tasty meals for him too. With a stomach that is never full, he eats his meals and escapes to the other tables for their offerings. Today I am with a dear friend, Sue Russell, an amazing animal advocate in her own right. With Quent, we sit down for a "quick" glass of wine and late lunch.

We didn't anticipate the Quentin factor. Every third person, even those with the stare-ahead sidewalk mask, stops to pet Quent. A good number have seen him on TV. Many tell us about their own pets. Quent eats it up. Lunch is cold and half-eaten, and it's now dinnertime. We order dinner. Between intermittent naps and total coddling by San Martin's owner—"Does Quentin want or need anything?"— Quent metamorphoses into Swifty Lazar at the "21"; he's actually table-hopping, schmoozing, begging for haute cuisine at one of the city's better restaurants. Sue

Quent enjoying his bone from the John Walsh Show at the W New York.

Photo by Randy Grim.

is a fellow animal person and Quent can tell animal people a mile away. He loves her. It's near midnight. After our second bottle of wine we all crawl back to the hotel. Quent still wants to party.

Prior to reentering the swank hotel we all stand outside and I have a smoke. The lobby looks crowded and I feel a bit anxious. My Midwest naiveté surfaces when two attractive women approach and gush over Quent. They gush for a long time, causing more anxiety for me. Finally, the pretty ladies are gone and we race to our rooms, sprinting past the lobby, and call it an evening.

Sue later informs me the two nice, gushing ladies were "ladies of the night."

"Ohhhh, you mean hookers?"

I was glad Quentin has a way of not caring about human stereotypes—like all dogs, he is just keen on the loving attention. If only mankind could master this basic instinct.

The following is a sampling of the emails and letters I have received since Quentin has become part of my life:

Dear Randy,
I read a story about Quentin and was led to your website and book . . . therefore reading a little about you and your journey. I just wanted to send this note to tell

you how moved I am at your courage and compassion. I am almost afraid to read the new book just released, because I feel that I am not strong enough to read the horror stories. I very much want to read it to understand how you got to where you are. My dream in this life is to rescue the innocent animals that are destroyed by us (mean and selfish) humans.

Nothing I read explained what will become of Quentin. I hope he has a good home.

God bless you in your work and your life. You've made a great difference on this planet.

Gordon and Betty Moore Foundation

Dear Randy,

Just wanted to say thank you for being such a wonderful person! The message of Quentin will make people more aware of how many wonderful dogs are being euthanized, and hopefully make people start adopting and fostering more!!!! I was recently put on the board of directors, and now the executive board of directors, at our local county shelter, Kent County Humane Society, Chestertown,

Photo by Randy Grim.

Two of Quentin's many fans, Sally Kim and Joan Higgins, visiting with him in New York.

Maryland. I only agreed to do it because I intend to make a difference. I will not be one of the members who sit on their butts and try to look important. I have been involved in their Mutt Strutt for about four years now, and always raised the most money (that is why they asked me to be on the board). I want to be hands-on in everything I can (time permitting). You are an inspiration to us all. I have ordered your book and can't wait to read it. Keep up the good work!
Thanks, Mary

Dear Randy,
Looks like precious Quentin will have the best home he could possibly get—with Randy Grim! And it looks like there may be changes in the works at the city pound!
(And with Randy and Quentin's travels: Here's God at work turning that which was horrendous and despicable into something helpful and good!) The result is progress for the animals!
Carol

Randy,
I first saw the story while I was at home at lunchtime yesterday on KSDK. But I also saw the report on WB last night at 9:00 and just wanted to let you know what a great job I thought you did during the interview. Most often, when a dog story makes the news it is because of animal abuse and usually has a tragic ending. It's so wonderful to have a dog story with a happy ending (happy is quite an understatement!).
I wonder who taught Quentin to hold his breath???
Jim

I saw the story of Quentin on the John Walsh Show today. I found your website to see what your organization is all about. I'm putting a donation to your Rescue Group in the mail today. We need many more people like you. I wish all people considered their pets as family members, as I do. If they did, there wouldn't be so much abuse.
Keep up the good work!
Kathy

SEVEN

Poster Child

MY BACKYARD IS A CROSS BETWEEN DOG-DESTROYED gardens with flowers pleading for mercy and a jungle gym. Squeaky toys and railroad ties envelop the grassy areas. A wall of large ornamental rocks holds up the unsightly garden. A small pond, doubling as the largest water bowl in America, marks the center of the courtyard. All my kids love it outside; I on the other hand wave a white flag of defeat almost every time I step out.

The rain starts, and herding them all inside is no easy task. Every time there's a downpour, the courtyard floods to murky depths of a minimum of six inches. Half my crew have "dainty" paws and need me to lug them in so their feet never touch the sopping ground, but then there is Quentin, half dog and half Mark Spitz. If he can survive the Gasconade, a pool of water is no match . . . or is it?

Everyone is inside but the lone Quent. I really have no time for this as I'm scheduled to talk with a St. Louis alderman on the phone about hiring a veterinarian for the city pound, so more humane ways than the gas chamber can be used to euthanize unwanted animals.

Standing on the flight of stairs that leads to dryness, I see the tan Wonder Dog doing his balance beam routine on the railroad ties. Agile and with controlled precision, he leaps with the grace of a Russian gymnast from one tie to the next. I score him a perfect "10" as I get soaked.

"Quentin, come on—get in here," I yell. "I gotta make a phone call. Come on!"

He gives me one quick head cock and a smirk and does another acrobatic leap. Now I am pissed and very wet.

"QUENTIN, NOW!" I scream. The backyard steps have transformed into a dock as the water rises. He gives me the "you are no fun" look and starts to prance to the edge of what looks like Lake Michigan.

"Quent, you gotta swim it buddy, I am not going in." I repeat this over and over to my little athlete. He takes a drink from the growing lake, ignoring my waterlogged pleas.

His torpedo-framed body backs up from the water's edge. He is going to do it. "Come on!" I urge.

And the sprint begins and then the aquatic leap into the deepest area of the pool of water. But he isn't coming towards me. Playing in the water with a soaked squeaky toy, he discounts me completely.

Oh lordy be, what the heck is he doing?

The dog paddle is what he is doing. He is in his own little water world of toys and ignoring his guardian! I have no choice. I must brave the stormy elements and go in and snare him.

Picture chasing a piece of paper caught in a vigorous gust of wind and you have an accurate image of me trying to catch Quentin in the water. He thinks we are playing a twisted game of Marco Polo or some other type of water diversion. I can almost grab his curled beacon of a tail and I reach with every fiber of my blundering human body. I collapse into the lake face first as he paddles away at a breakneck speed onto the waterless stairs. He stands there looking at me all high and mighty and I swear I hear him say, "Come on! Get in here, you fool!"

I spit out scum water like a malfunctioning fountain and grin. I hear the phone ringing. I have missed the important call. I hurry up the stairs while Quentin toots a wake of gas in front of me and we head towards the receiver. Soaked and out of breath, I begin to dial. At least when you're on the phone, the person you're talking with can't see you.

"It will never happen; it just isn't a priority. We don't even have the funding to test for venereal disease," says the St. Louis alderman. This is his response to the idea of hiring a veterinarian at the city pound to replace the gas chamber. With Quent's ordeal gaining nationwide attention, I naively thought that the city would be more than willing to ban its now-infamous gas chamber, or would at least be embarrassed into banning it.

VD? If you have VD, the test is the least of your worries. It should be the person's financial responsibility—and not my tax dollars—to pay for the test. Humans who exploit animals know the mantra by heart: Humans are superior because of our ability to reason (people who know animals know that's a crock). But politics and animals mix about as well as oil and water. I understood the alderman's point: St. Louis City officials will not budget a dime for a more humane method of animal control. But if you get VD, you're in luck. Why do innocents always get the raw end of the deal?

He survived the
GAS CHAMBER
Millions of animals aren't so lucky.

Quentin,
The Miracle Dog

Adopt & Save a Life
Be a Guardian, **Not an Owner.**

www.StrayRescue.org
Stray Rescue of St. Louis

www.idausa.org
In Defense of Animals **IDA**

One of the numerous billboards and posters on which Quentin appears as national spokesdog with In Defense of Animals.

I don't hang up without asking the alderman about making other changes in our current animal ordinances, especially changing the wording from "owner" to "guardian." Many may think that this is just silly. But I see the good ol' boy, utilitarian view—and its results—every day. Something's got to change.

The guardian campaign, sponsored by In Defense of Animals (IDA), has been gaining strength and backing across the country. According to IDA, our changing attitudes toward animals are reflected in the language that we use to write and speak about them. I agree.

Surveys indicate that the vast majority of people with animals in their care think of them as family members. "Animal guardian" or "animal caretakers" are respectful terms that are consistent with public sentiment. As we use kinder terms, our children will absorb the message that cats, dogs, and other animals are living beings that depend on people for long-term care and protection. And it is catching on; thirteen cities, one county and the State of Rhode Island have changed the wording in their ordinances to the word "guardian."

In a recent interview with the *Pet Press* in Los Angeles, I summed it up like this:

I don't feel comfortable using phrases like "my pets" or being "their owner." The word "guardian" makes the connection of respect, love, and care that I share and owe to my kids (my preferred wording of "my pets"). Being an animal guardian helps ensure that the mindset of our society—the mindset that condones discarding the rights of animals or being part of a throwaway society when it comes to all living things—is simply not acceptable. We can't just pick and choose what we want to discard in this world, especially when we created such a horrible environment for the animals. To me, we should try to save them all—and not just save them but prevent, too. We have to try to change the way people think. Quentin ended up at the pound simply because his people were moving to an apartment that didn't accept dogs. That's such a lame excuse. Animals are not to be disposed of, but cared for and respected, guarded from harm's way. A world of animals and guardians is my own personal nirvana. A man can dream.[1]

Quentin is now a vital part of this dream.

IDA has been very supportive of Stray Rescue in the past and more recently with Quentin's miraculous fortitude. The next call I make is to Dr. Elliot Katz at IDA to get some advice and to RSVP for the upcoming IDA Guardian Award presentation ceremony. I am scared and embarrassed about receiving the award, but

For the past twenty years, In Defense of Animals has been at the forefront of the fight for animal rights. The year 2003 was no exception. During that year IDA was instrumental in:

- ending the hideous mother deprivation experiments of Mark Laudenslager;
- coordinating protests and educational events against the cruelties of the vivisection, fur, puppy mill, dog meat, agriculture and entertainment industries;
- rescuing thousands of abused and abandoned animals;
- protecting and giving sanctuary to chimpanzees in Cameroon, Africa, and abused animals in rural Mississippi; and
- helping San Francisco become the seventh U.S. city to recognize the importance and benefits of animal guardianship.

IDA has been a constant and powerful force, a protector of and voice for our animal friends.

am awed and honored as well. My own personal hero, Jane Goodall, also will receive an award. I am no Jane Goodall. I feel very undeserving. But it's natural for Quentin to be honored and become a symbol of hope—the poster child—for all homeless animals. We discuss his future and I listen to Dr. Katz's words of wisdom on how to make the changes in the local ordinances.

Dr. Katz and I agree to promote Quentin's plight by officially making him the poster dog at the Guardian awards. We discuss logistics about bringing Quent to Los Angeles. It appears as if another trip for Quent is forthcoming.

Next, I schedule a meeting with the mayor of St. Louis and place additional calls to further discuss the current ordinances.

It's strange, but I believe Quentin knew he'd be the poster dog long before any of us did. He knew his destiny the day he walked out of the chamber with his tail up. It shows in every fiber of his being . . . except at home.

Quentin and Hannah's friendship has blossomed into a full-blown love affair. He can do anything to her, from climbing on her head to stealing her treats, at which he's become a master. Hannah worships Quent, and to this day I am astounded by their alliance. After all, Hannah used to be the Queen Bitch of the house.

With three new brothers and one sister/girlfriend, Quent is settling into the Grim Household just fine. Horsey, the Rottweiler/shepherd mix whom I unfortunately named over martinis, is the only jealous one. Horsey reminds Quent of his seniority via discreet growls, signifying that he is an original pack member. Bear, the wise old black chow who's king of the castle, enjoys Quentin's youth and exuberance—as long as Quent respects Bear's alpha-ness. Then there is twenty-year-old Petey, aka "Yoda." Weighing only four pounds, Petey is old and nearing the end of his bighearted Shitzu-mix life. Quentin shows him the utmost respect, gentle care, and kindness. This is Quent's new family and he seems to love it, especially since the rules of my house are that there are no rules. Dogs just get to be dogs.

It's not surprising that when the day comes for us to meet the mayor of St. Louis, my clan declares anarchy. I find the only sport jacket I own and discover a sleeve missing. I opt for a regular button-down shirt. Hannah and Quent play tug-of-war with the amputated sleeve while I finish getting dressed and rehearsing my case as to why we need a veterinarian at the pound and not a chamber. Knowing the mayor will only care about financial figures, I must convince him that this

Quentin watching over Petey during his last days.

Photo by Randy Grim.

proposal can save money. How can he resist Quent's imploring face, and, despite all that dog has endured, his wagging tail? How can he not empathize with the living hell this little guy endured—in a St. Louis "shelter"? Surely, the mayor is going to agree with my position.

Built in 1904, City Hall has a ghostlike, gothic feel to it. Jenn and Quentin flank my sides as the news media tape us walking up the stairs. I am impressed with the splendor and grandness as we approach the mayor's office. Quentin, as if programmed, goes into his time-to-pose mode while I become a bundle of nerves.

Quentin models with the mayor, his wife, and staff members. He absorbs the attention like a sponge. All the while I rehearse in my head what I must emphasize at the meeting. As usual in situations like this, I feel that sweat 'stache forming on my upper lip.

I am overwhelmed as we sit down. There are seven or more officials seated alongside the mayor in the lush "living room" area of his office. Quent goes exploring the office as the meeting starts.

"Well, um, I wanted to see about hiring a vet on staff for the city," I begin, my voice quavering. "Here, let me pass these out." We distribute the nifty folders we made that contain information supporting my point about a vet and the guardian campaign. By the looks on their faces, I sense that they regard the folders like a bad homework assignment. The mayor never opens his.

The sweat 'stache now spreads to my brow, but I cannot panic. I must make my case and get them to look at this information. I need help, and fast—and help arrives. Quentin is actually sitting in the chair behind the mayor's desk, looking as if he's running our city. Everyone laughs. That moment of comic relief somewhat alleviates my anxiety and allows me to speak more fluently.

"If we had a vet we could actually save money," I say. "Besides making the gas chamber a secondary means of euthanasia, the vet could observe impounded animals, give the appropriate care, spay and neuter, provide care for the police dogs and horses, and do education and outreach."

I sense that I'm losing them. "It's all in your packet," I say, giving up.

"It won't happen. I have to cut the budget this year," the mayor replies. "Now if you can raise the funds yourself, then that would be different."

Yeah, right! I think, but I keep a weak smile on my face.

The conversation moves to the Animal House Fund, designed to raise money through private donations for a new animal regulation facility. If enough money can be raised, I think, perhaps a vet can be included in the facility's budget. I completely support this effort and am willing to do anything I can to help.

"Let's utilize Quentin to attract more donations," I suggest. The troubling part of the entire conversation is that I feel my ideas are falling upon deaf ears.

The mayor seems just fine about gassing the animals. I want so badly to blurt out, "Mr. Mayor, you say you love animals. You showed me a picture of your rescued dog and you are looking Quentin in the eye, yet I feel as if you couldn't give a damn. Maybe you should go observe some of the executions." But nooo, security officers certainly would kick us out of City Hall and our names would be put on some sort of

City Hall blacklist. Instead, I nod often and drift off into space, wondering how I can get through to this man. I do believe he is a good man with an impossible job. Prioritizing a city budget is an arduous task, but I still wonder why my nifty packet seems so low on his list. *Come on, Quentin, do something!* But Quentin offers no assistance—he's too busy sniffing in the mayor's trash.

Photo by Jenn Foster.

*Peter Falk, Randy and Quentin enjoy-
ing a night out in Hollywood.*

Before we leave, I discuss the guardian campaign. They seem more receptive and attentive, particularly when I say the project shouldn't cost the city a dime. Quentin poses for more pictures, and we leave, feeling defeated and deflated.

As we descend the grand spiral staircase to the exit, I ask Jenn what she thinks about what just occurred. Jenn hits the nail right on the head.

"A glorified photo op," Jenn says, shaking her head.

"They don't really let you state your case; it's like talking to Muppets with stuffing for brains," I add, depressed. Quent just wags his tail. He enjoyed playing mayor for a day.

Back home on the bed with my gang, I reflect on everything—Quentin's role as the poster dog, the chamber, the guardian campaign. I conclude that I can't give up. That's a valuable lesson I learned from my miracle son.

Feeling courageous, the next morning I phone Phyllis Young, an animal-loving alderman who is willing to meet about the guardian campaign and sponsor the change. Another City Hall meeting is set; I can hardly wait. This is sarcasm here.

Later in the day I check my e-mails and discover one from the IDA. It includes a prototype of the new national Quentin poster that will be unveiled at the awards ceremony. It looks great—and I am rejuvenated.

PART THREE

EIGHT

Home at Last

MORE MEDIA. QUENT AND I ARE WORKING WITH THE local Fox television affiliate for a long piece to be aired during the coveted sweeps period. The day starts off like so many have recently—prying cameras in our house.

"It will be kind of a 'day in the life of' type of piece, or I should say, '*days* in the life of,'" Paul Schankman of Fox 2 News explains over the phone.

Quent always is ready for this; Dad always dreads it.

"Can we come over now?" Schankman inquires.

"Sure, sure, the house is a bit of a mess—I have a zoo," I respond halfheartedly.

That horrible *Twelve Days of Christmas* doorbell chimes, announcing the arrival of the Fox crew.

"Randy, we want to film Quentin at home, what his day is like and all, and do an interview today too, with you," says Schankman.

"No problem. Prepare yourselves," I laugh.

It always is funny to watch a cameraman and reporter, or any unseasoned animal lover, enter my house. First, they have to ascend a lengthy staircase flanked with resting fat cats who don't budge, and then enter the second floor of hysterical barking and jubilation. One thing is for sure—my dogs love people and always get energized when visitors come knocking.

The Fox team is tackled by the pack, with Quentin leading the attack by jumping on and kissing our guests.

"You're the man who talks to dogs, but your dogs are, well . . ." Schankman trails off.

I do understand dogs, and I love them enough to let them be dogs, even though that means putting up with behavior that other people might call "trouble." "My kids are so well trained—NOT. I have few rules." We both laugh.

"Let's start with some footage of everyone playing in the yard," he suggests.

"You got it." My crew is more than willing to wreak havoc outside anytime.

71

Quentin bolts like a gazelle out the back door, down the vertical stairs, leaps across the small pond and races across a stretch of overused, mutilated grass. The others follow in the spirited chase. They are no match for Quentin's slender, agile frame and speed. He thoroughly enjoys the chase, knowing that he can only be caught on his terms.

"He is so fast. Getting a shot of this will be hard," says the Fox cameraman.

It's amusing to watch the Fox crew's attempt to shoot the cat-and-mouse game. I take a front-row seat on the steps.

In no time, Schankman and the cameraman are looking decidedly defeated—they soon raise the white flag of surrender. The dogs retreat inside for some homey shots. I'm convinced that Quentin is just toying with the crew—the John Walsh program redux.

"Well, I have to feed them, so this should be some fun footage and should calm them down," I say as I lay out nearly a dozen metal bowls.

"Quentin has to eat in the bathroom, though," I say. "He is such a chowhound and a tad rude that he annoys the others while they eat. But he will learn."

Photo by Randall Solomon.

Quentin hanging out in the backyard.

Schankman laughs—Quent spins like a top with excitement as I place his food in the bathroom and shut the door, leaving the cameraman in the john with him.

Next, the kids charge up the stairs to the third floor and spring onto my bed, and I get to do a pleasurable interview for a change, in bed. Hannah is glued to my stomach and Quent positions himself between my legs. The interview is about to start and I can't help but think that since Quentin came into my life, my bedroom has seen more action than in the past seventeen years! I need a life.

Schankman stands at the foot of the bed with his notepad. With camera rolling, he begins asking questions.

"Do the other dogs sense that there is something different about him?" he asks.

"Yes, they all accepted him immediately like he has lived here all of his life. I have had hundreds of dogs come through my house, and it has always been a huge adjustment because Hannah never accepts any of them. This is so meant to be."

And I say this to Quent, too. He gives me a puppy kiss. I melt and ask my pooch, "Are you gonna help Daddy change some laws?"

I get another kiss.

Schankman then asks how home is different from being in public. As Hannah stares into the camera lens, I explain.

"He is goofy like this, plays, and hangs in bed. But in public he has to turn on his celebrity status and help educate and show people he is a wonderful dog, and dogs like him die in the millions every year," I tell him. Quentin inches close to my face, as if he knows I am talking about him.

Schankman then asks if Quentin likes to travel, and I explain how he loves to travel, meet people, loves first class (as does Dad now), is great with children, and how he needs to know that I am close by.

Quentin now stands on my chest, towering over me. The camera moves in and I ask Quent, "Are you enjoying standing over Dad? You like it up there?"

I speak to Schankman again. "When he travels, he eats it up. Gosh, on the plane he got six turkey sandwiches. Passengers give up their food for him; everyone just wants to meet him."

Schankman's final question: "Do you have a feeling his fifteen minutes of fame are up?"

"I think, you know, his fifteen minutes would already be up. We are, like, on eighteen minutes and it's still not up. He has a lifetime of educating; he will always be remembered as the dog who survived the gas chamber. There is no such thing as fifteen minutes for Quentin."

I look in my beautiful dog's eyes and then say, "Too bad he doesn't know how to do the laundry. That would help out a lot." Schankman and the cameraman laugh.

We take some shots in the park, my favorite being Quentin lifting his leg to pee and me doing the same, mocking him. Schankman tells me he will see us on the flight to Los Angeles for the awards. Fox News is documenting the whole trip, along with representatives for PAX TV's *It's a Miracle* show. This should be interesting.

Next on the agenda is a meeting at City Hall. This time, however, Quentin won't be there to calm my nerves. This meeting will not be a photo op with Quent. It will consist of Alderman Phyllis Young, Rich Stevson of St. Louis Animal Regulation, and the city's attorney. With my rock, Jenn, by my side, we depart for this rigid rendezvous, armed with information packets for all participants.

"What are your sources for the surveys on the term 'guardian' making such a difference?" the attorney asks as he begins regarding his packet.

I start to explain, but Stevson interrupts. He's defensive, and isn't listening. "We are one of the most progressive animal controls in the country," he says, quickly, and "You are even too afraid to walk in the back of Animal Control because you get so upset." Yep, I am guilty of having feelings here, and I then do something I regret later: I explode like a stick of dynamite. I am so pissed off because everyone seems to be missing the point. I'm not here to slam Animal Control; I'm not here to pick battles. I recall cursing a little. . . . I am not a politician, would never want to be one, but why in the hell do these City Hall meetings never focus on why I am there? Thank God, the voice of reason finally speaks.

"I don't see the big deal here; we can make the changes when we overhaul the ordinances," says Phyllis Young. She's calm and direct. She asks Stevson how long this will take, and hopefully after the first of the year it can be accomplished. Stevson still seems agitated.

Feeling a little embarrassed, I apologize for my outburst. If Quentin were with us, he would have diffused the situation by raiding the trash, sitting at the table or, knowing him, passing out the nifty packets himself.

Stevson and I go way back. At one time we hated each other. To me, he was nothing more than an animal killer with no heart, and to him, I probably was nothing more than a liberal animal activist. But over time, more than ten years, I began

Quentin and Randy with Rich Stevson of St. Louis Animal Regulation, Paul Schankman of Fox 2 TV, and Troy Lea of Best Friends Animal Sanctuary.

to understand what he faces every day and started to understand his positions and decisions. He wasn't the evil prince of darkness that I thought. We actually became friends over the years. Animal Regulation has made some great strides, from allowing rescue organizations to pull death row inmates from the pound to implementing strong penalties for irresponsible pet guardians. Sure, we butt heads periodically and passionately, but we always work it out and seem to be able to nurture a better relationship through our battles. I guess what I am saying is that he's not on my hit list. It just appears that way sometimes.

Once again we exit the mammoth City Hall building, and once again I ask Jenn her thoughts on the meeting. Jenn gets everything, and everybody, on the first take.

"Well, that was pure hell," she says as we rush through the doors.

"Yeah, I am all fired up, but at least the guardian wording looks like it will get changed," I say. "Let's hope they stick to it. Could have used Quentin on this one for sure."

Back home, safe from the recent fray, I let the dogs out to play. Quentin charges the back gate and, sniffing through the cracks on the other side, is a stray brindle pit bull. Everyone barks and growls except Quent. I rush out and grab the notorious bully, Hannah, and put her in the house. I open the back gate into the city alley. Quent strolls out and greets the stray with the official dog hello—the butt sniff. He licks the pit's muzzle and I swear he telepathically says, *Come on in, the water's just fine.* The stray pit, although scared and skeletal, walks into the backyard as I close the gate.

Bear and Horse greet our guest in a more dominant manner, trying to mount him. I shoo them off the poor guy while Quent just stands guard next to him. After twenty minutes of greetings, they play the chase game, with Quent making sure he is the target. Quent probably thinks this new kid will give him more of a run for his money than the usual players.

Everyone follows me into the house. Hannah is in her crate, acting like Hannah-bal Lecter trying to attack her victim, the new guy. Quentin politely gathers his rope toy and lays it at the stray dog's paws. I am amazed. Quent empathized, I could tell. He is the only one of my crew to have such a mature, loving reaction to this misfit from the streets. I am so proud of him, again.

I load the emaciated stray, now with a full belly, and Quentin into my car. Off we head to the Stray Rescue shelter, where one day he also will find his forever home. On the drive back home, I realize that Quentin has settled in for good, that he is now part of my life and my family. He knows it too. He curls up on my lap, content in the knowledge that he has just rescued a dog. In a way, I guess he did.

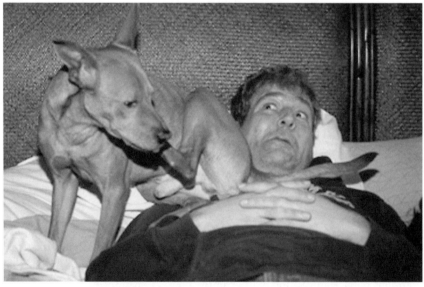

Dad and Quentin relaxing (?) at home.

Photo by Donna Lochmann.

NINE

The Bottom Line

QUENTIN'S RESURRECTION IS A MIRACLE. BUT HIS ordeal isn't the only one that made headlines in 2003. The veil, the myth of peaceably "putting dogs and cats to sleep" as we destroy massive numbers of dogs and cats in shelters in the United States, is gradually being lifted. Similar horror stories have surfaced; most don't make the headlines. In writing this book, I've talked with many shelter workers who recount mishaps and purely abusive and neglectful situations occurring almost daily in our fractured shelter system. Many stories are horrendous: puppies destroyed through suffocation in coffee cans, dogs bleeding to death or killing each other while behind bars. This is difficult for us to hear about, especially if we love animals.

In December 2003, one particular story caught my eye and freaked me out; it parallels Quentin's yarn. It happened in Perth Amboy, New Jersey. A 45-year-old animal control officer, William Paul, not only botched the euthanasia of a five-year-old female shepherd mix but also facilitated the unplanned torture of this unfortunate pooch.

This poor dog's hell began with the woman who brought her to the Perth Amboy shelter. Paul told the woman the dog would have to be euthanized because of lack of space. This woman apparently did not care that her dog of five years was about to be destroyed. She just walked away. Like Quentin's "owners," she was moving to a place that didn't accept dogs. Instead of trying to find a home that did, or place her dog herself, she opted to kill her loyal companion.

Paul gave the dog a lethal injection, listened for a heartbeat and then threw her body into a dumpster where it was compacted with trash on a garbage truck.

The next day, a landfill worker spotted the dog as she poked her head out of the plastic trash bag that encased her body at the rear of the dump truck. An East Brunswick animal control officer was called to the scene. The dog then was taken to a local kennel.

"It's evident that he didn't use sufficient drugs to put the animal down, and it's evident that he did not properly listen for a heartbeat in a quiet environment," said Joseph Biermann of the New Jersey Society for the Prevention of Cruelty to Animals in an interview with the *Home News Tribune* of East Brunswick.[1]

Abandoned at the pound, injected with drugs, thrown in a dumpster and compacted in a truck, the dog still managed to wag her tail when she arrived at the kennel.

Perth Amboy city officials have suspended Paul and plan to fire him. If he is found guilty of criminal charges he may have to pay $1,000 and spend six months in jail. And by the way, it is legal in New Jersey to throw a euthanized dog in the trash. It is odd that city officials just blame Paul when, with lethal injection, the drug's dosage is determined by weight and the shelter doesn't even own a scale. It's the system. The same officials denouncing Paul are the ones who are supposed to be responsible for making sure that competent, compassionate people and procedures are in place at every shelter for every animal. Despite regulations, despite talk, what goes on in too many local "shelters" is botched and neglectful. Dogs can't talk. For too many local governments, these animals, and how they are treated, aren't even on the radar screen. Complaints, when they are registered, are ignored or, at best, humored.

The Jersey wonder dog is now adopted and will never face this hell again. Was she the only one to suffer in Paul's eighteen years of employment there? I have serious doubts. How about his supervisors? And is $1,000 punishment enough? Well, if you made it this far into the book, I think you would agree that the answer is *absolutely not*. Accountability is about as common as an overfunded shelter. The public doesn't get to see what goes on behind closed doors. Facility inspectors usually provide plenty of notice to operators to allow them to present the facade that all is well. The assumption that people who work at animal control care about the animals in their care doesn't hold much water. They are government employees with a job, and loving animals isn't a requirement for employment.

Maybe one day Quentin will be able to meet his soul sister.

Back in St. Louis another shocker hit the papers. A pit bull named Candyman had saved his human family of seven—and their other smaller dog—from a fire. Candyman had the intelligence and heart to warn and wake every family member, and even dragged one of the children to safety. To repay this unlikely hero for saving their lives, the family took him to the Gasconade pound—the same pound Quentin survived—the one with the overworked gas chamber. *Thanks Candyman. We lived, now you die.*

The last picture of Candyman taken as he relaxes at the home of his rescuer, Gale Frey.

Although family members were upset about taking Candyman to the pound, they said they could not have dogs at their new home—but they were able to keep the smaller dog. Once again, the family dog, the one who had rescued the *entire* family, was not deemed worthy enough to be part of the move. The local media reported Candyman's heroic deed but failed to mention that his ultimate reward was a trip to the Gasconade gas chamber. What is wrong with this picture?

Candyman's story does not have a tragic conclusion. A rescuer, Gale Frey, knew of his plight and saved Candyman from the pound. She renamed him Harry. As of this writing, Harry has found a home in Chicago, the kind of loving home a hero deserves.

Ordeals like Quentin's, Candyman's and many other kindred shelter animals' can be prevented. We must no longer accept killing as the method of containing the pet overpopulation problem. Irresponsible pet guardianship creates the problem, and unfortunately the innocent suffer. The no-kill movement is gaining strength and acceptance every year.

Ed Boks, Executive Director of New York City Animal Care and Control, summed up the no-kill movement to me as follows:

> The recent societal awakening to the realities of the human/animal bond and the intrinsic value of all living creatures has given birth to a national movement called "no-kill." Although the values espoused by this new movement offer nothing new to most of us in the animal control

Ed Boks with Quentin in New York.

field, it is ironic that the term "no-kill" seems to offend so many of my colleagues in that field.

I submit that we in the animal control field should not shun or resent this new movement. On the contrary, we should embrace it. This movement belongs to us as much as it belongs to anyone. No-kill is nothing more than a manifestation of our own industry's evolution from regulatory rabies control programs to progressive animal care and control programs, with an ancillary rabies-monitoring component. Just as we were successful in substantially reducing the risk of rabies in our communities, so I believe we can be key players in substantially reducing euthanasia of healthy, adoptable pets.[2]

Officials of Maddie's Fund, a multimillion-dollar foundation that funds community collaborations with the goal of ending the killing, offered another perspective:
As much as anything, no-kill is a rallying cry; a slogan that defines a movement. The term "no-kill" clearly and powerfully protests the status

quo, that being the killing of millions of savable animals in our nation's animal shelters every year. At the same time, it describes a new approach to animal sheltering and a new commitment to saving lives within animal welfare organizations.[3]

And the rallying cry is working. Animal welfare advocates in the state of Utah have striven for completely no-kill status under the stewardship of Best Friends Animal Sanctuary. According to that organization, the statewide coalition now includes ninety veterinary hospitals, twenty-five no-kill organizations, fifty-seven animal control agencies, and two traditional shelters. The coalition's campaign, "No More Homeless Pets," began in 2000. In 2003, adoptions from rescue groups were up 250 percent over the numbers in 1999; adoptions from shelters were up 14 percent for the same years.[4] No-kill advocates acknowledge there will be animals that are too sick, aggressive, or injured to be adopted out.

Plutarch wrote: "The obligations of law and equity reach only to mankind, but kindness and benevolence should be extended to the creatures of every species, and these will flow from the breast of a true man." (*Moralia*)

Thomas Edison once said: "Non-violence leads to the highest ethics, which is the goal of all evolution. Until we stop harming all other living beings, we are savages." (*Harper's Magazine*, 1890)

Albert Schweitzer said: "Our civilization lacks humane feeling. We are humans who are insufficiently humane! We must realize that and seek to find a new spirit. We have lost sight of this ideal because we are solely occupied with thoughts of men instead of remembering that our goodness and compassion should extend to all creatures." (Letter to Aida Fleming, 1959)

Harriet Beecher Stowe, who worked so nobly against slavery, wrote: "I and my daughter and my husband have been regarded as almost fanatical in our care of animals wherever we have been. . . . I for my part am ready to do anything that can benefit the cause. It's a matter of taking the side of the weak against the strong, something the best people have always done." (Letter to Henry Bruge, Nov. 6, 1877)

San Francisco, the first city in the United States to achieve no-kill status, serves as a model city. Aggressive spay and neuter programs and the formation of coalitions were key to reducing the intake of the animals that normally would end up in the shelter system. As a result, San Francisco shelters saw an increase in donations and adopters. Like the Guardian Campaign, it is astounding what happens when society decides changes must be made.

What is needed to change things? In addition to actively working for no-kill status, we also must have the heart and the will to enact change in our societal values. Our dogs will stand by us when we don't have a dime, when nobody else will. Yet, for the slightest of reasons, we throw them away like old radios. As a society, we must respect and value their lives. Our most noted thinkers throughout history have known this, from Seneca and Pythagoras to Thomas Edison and Mark Twain.

I can only briefly touch on the no-kill movement in this writing. The topic is complex and intricate, but it is relevant to Quentin and the shelter system. If Quent's original guardians had really thought about his fate or had the educational resources readily available to them, he may never have entered the chamber.

No-kill was knocked down in St. Louis, surprisingly by one of the wealthiest of all animal shelters in the world. The Humane Society of Missouri (HSM) has an $11 million facility that resembles a lavish shopping mall and boasts an annual budget of more than $8 million. Upper management views me as the anti-Christ. I can only think it is fear of change that makes officials so anti-Randy, anti-Stray Rescue and anti-no-kill. HSM has the most money and kills the most pets in our state. They refuse to talk despite any olive branch attempts on my part. HSM's complete lack of cooperation is the primary reason why our local animal welfare agencies' applications for Maddie's Fund support and other grants are turned down. Philanthropists like to see collaborations—HSM makes all of us in animal welfare look bad.

I recently asked a comrade, Merrit Clifton, editor of *Animal People*, his thoughts on the subject. All I could say to myself was "wow" when I read his response. Here is an excerpt:

> If you keep dogs and cats in a facility that looks like a jail and smells like a cesspool, dogs and cats all over town will be treated like prisoners on a chain gang, because the condition of your facility sends the message that you think this is okay.

> If you treat dogs and cats as if they are honored guests, the community standards will rise to your standard. This, too, has been proved time and again.

Finally, you need care-for-life sanctuaries as a backup for the animals who cannot be adopted out because many people will not bring a dog or cat to a shelter if they think the animal might be killed. Instead, they will abandon the animal somewhere "to give him a chance" or "give her a chance." That animal may then contribute to the breeding population of street dogs and feral cats.

People give up pets for all sorts of reasons. Whether or not we think the reasons are "valid," giving up pets is a fact of life that must be accommodated. It must be understood that many of these pets are given up not because they are not loved, but because desperate people feel they have no choice: they have lost their job, lost a home, an animal has bitten or scratched a child, the spouse hates the animal, the landlord is threatening to evict them, or someone has died and the pet-keeper is so depressed he or she just can't cope.

If these people feel the pet is going to either find a home or be well looked after at a sanctuary, they will bring the animal into the adoption-and-care network. The animal will not end up having "accidental" litters out on the streets, further contributing to the homeless animal problem.

Animal control agencies that can respond immediately to nuisance animal complaints and act as a dog-and-cat lost-and-found are very nice to have—but they are not what it takes to end pet overpopulation and shelter killing.

Full-service humane societies that can provide emergency veterinary care, do humane education, do animal rescue, and investigate cruelty complaints are also nice to have. Yet they are not what it takes to end pet overpopulation and shelter killing.

A community placing the first emphasis on developing animal control agencies and full-service humane societies, in short, is going in the wrong direction.

It all depends on which way you go from here. Go the right way, and you can soon be leading the world.[5]

No-kill promotes educational programs, spay and neuter programs for the poor, progressive adoption events and, most importantly, community involvement and hope. I am often asked what one person can do. My answer is: *a lot*. A story like Quentin's should compel all animal lovers to unite and work toward one common goal—to stop the killing.

What One Person Can Do!

- Spay and neuter your own pet and support community low-cost de-sexing programs. Men seem to have the hardest time with this. For some reason, they think by neutering their dog they are ridding him of some twisted human form of manhood. (I actually think men worry they may be next.)
- Stop buying from pet stores. With close to six million companion animals destroyed in our shelters and millions more dying on our streets each year, a great alternative is adopting at your local shelters. Don't head to the mall for your next pet; go to your local shelter. Puppy millers fill pet stores with sickly animals and directly affect the pet overpopulation problem. I know there is a demand for purebreds; most shelters have about 30 percent purebreds. Shop there if all possible.
- Tag and microchip the family pets. Stray Rescue gets at least thirty calls a day from guardians missing their pets. More than 75 percent are not chipped. Sadly, many are destroyed at local shelters before the guardians can claim them. Chips and proper identification, such as tags, can prevent such needless tragedy.
- Stop chaining the dog to the doghouse or leaving him in the yard all the time. First of all, this isn't much fun for the dog. More importantly, however, the dog may escape—or worse, be stolen—and end up as another somber statistic. Dogs are pack animals. Let them be part of the family pack—indoors.
- Volunteer at your local shelter. Help and support are always needed. If you don't have the time, then send a donation or collect needed items such as food and blankets.
- Support laws that substantially increase license fees for pets that have not been spayed or neutered. This gives guardians an incentive to sterilize their pets.
- Put your dog on the moving checklist. Tell your moving neighbor to do the same. If you can't keep your pet, find the dog or cat a home on your own and thereby avoid jeopardizing your pet's life by taking him to a shelter.
- Teach your children the use of the word "guardian" and teach compassion, for they are the next generation of animal welfare leaders and guardians.

TEN

Reaching for the Stars

The American Airlines Boeing 757 takes off for Los Angeles like it does every day, but this time it has precious cargo—Quentin and my mom are traveling with me. And—need I say it?—Fox 2 News cameras are also on board. They are focused on Quentin and me. Behind us are two of my friends and Stray Rescue volunteers, Gaynell Gallagher and Kelly Brinkman. Paul Schankman of Fox 2 News and my mom are seated across from us. Paul is by now part of the Stray Rescue family.

For Quentin, all of this is now old hat; he is the sophisticated traveler. Gasconade is in his distant past. Craning his small head, he gazes out the plane's window, allows passengers to pet him and take his picture, and laps up the affection he'd never had his first year of life. I, on the other hand, am a self-conscious mess. Anxiety isn't in my distant past; it's my ever-present companion. There is nothing worse than a camera pointed at you while you try to "act" normal, eat, or drink.

Gaynell slips me airline baby booze bottles to pour into my juice. She knows of my anxiety problems and I welcome the alcohol to numb my nerves. But self-anesthetization is out. Besides the cameras and an upcoming, star-studded ceremony where I will have to speak, there is a microphone attached to my body so the Fox crew can hear every word I say. That means no cussing or belching. The sweat 'stache forms between gulps of my doctored orange juice as I do the interview on the plane.

"Oh, he just loves all of this. He knows he is on a plane and knows when the meal service starts, too. I am always amazed at how he thinks everything through." And I simultaneously grab my drink, casually wipe the gathering sweat from my lip and continue to run on about how wonderful Quentin is.

Comforting as it is to have friends and family along, we all feel as if we are on a bizarre reality TV show that may require a rose ceremony when we land. Quentin is in Turkey Sandwich Heaven. At last count, he's had seven, and he's not slowing down. There's an underground railroad on this plane. Passengers fifteen rows back are finding ways of getting Quent all manner of goodies from their trays.

Food is a big motivator for Quent. I'm convinced the reason he loves to fly is the smorgasbord of food—when Quent sees a plane, he sees "All You Can Eat Buffet."

The plane lands and news crews and fanfare greet us. More photo ops, more interviews, more sweat 'staches for me, and I am out of juice. There's a car waiting, and we positively lunge into the backseat. Peace and quiet, but not for long.

THE SOUSSANA GROUP

468 NORTH CAMDEN DRIVE, SUITE 200
BEVERLY HILLS, CALIFORNIA 90210
TANY@THESOUSSANAGROUP.COM

310.860-5690 TEL
310.860-5600 FAX

For Immediate Release

Contact: Tany Soussana,
Shayna Emanuel
(310) 860-5690

IN DEFENSE OF ANIMALS
1st ANNUAL GUARDIAN AWARDS
NAMES RANDY GRIM AS LATEST HONOREE
AND MIRACLE DOG, QUENTIN, AS "POSTER CHILD"

SAVE THE DATE
Thursday, October 16, Hotel Casa del Mar, Santa Monica

(BEVERLY HILLS: September 26, 2003) – **In Defense of Animals (IDA)** adds to its distinguished line-up of honorees as names **Randy Grim**, founder of the **Stray Rescue of St. Louis**, to receive the prestigious Guardian Award while also naming **Quentin**, the miracle dog, as the organization's new **"Poster Child."** Both will be honored at the IDA's **1st Annual Guardian Awards** celebrity gala, scheduled on **October 16** at **Hotel Casa del Mar** in **Santa Monica, California**, it was announced today by IDA president and founder, **Dr. Elliot Katz**.

"It gives us great pride to present Randy Grim with our Guardian Award for his unyielding love, courage and dedication to saving St. Louis' most abused and abandoned dogs, and creating a new home for these lost dogs through his Stray Rescue of St. Louis," says Dr. Katz. "Every town should have more Randy Grims in their neighborhood, and we know our new 'Poster Child,' Quentin, would certainly agree."

Among other animal activist VIP's to be presented the Guardian Award at this special celebration, Grim is the latest recipient to be honored by the IDA with their Guardian Award for his outstanding achievement and lifetime devotion to animal rights, particularly with dogs. He will be joining the company of other honorees who currently include **Dr. Jane Goodall**, **Gretchen Wyler** and **Matt Gonzalez**. Grim garnered national praise for his unusual rescue of shelter dog, Quentin. Dubbed a "miracle dog," Quentin was gassed with other dogs, however was the only one to survive the gas chamber, and was soon after rescued by Grim.

"It is important that we keep all animals safe and protected from inhumane conduct, a tragedy which goes on everyday to innocent animals. If people on death row cannot get gassed because it's illegal, then why are animals not allowed the same humane treatment?" The subject of a new book, **The Man Who Talks to Dogs**, Grim further challenges, "I truly hope the recognition we receive turns into awareness for people to do the right thing. As a society we can no longer accept the fast exit for the sake of so-called animal control."

IN DEFENSE OF ANIMALS IS A NON-PROFIT, TAX-EXEMPT 501(C)(3) CORPORATION. TICKETS ARE $250. ALL PROCEEDS BENEFIT THE IDA, WHOSE POLICY IT IS TO CEASE USING LANGUAGE WHICH ACCEPTS THE CURRENT CONCEPT OF ANIMALS AS PROPERTY, COMMODITIES AND/OR THINGS. GUARDIANS DO NOT BUY OR SELL ANIMALS; INSTEAD THEY RESCUE AND ADOPT.

The limo whisks us—shelter volunteers, mean street rescuers, and an abandoned dog—away to a fancy restaurant to meet Tany Soussana, a top LA publicist who will help us get attention for the street dog issue for the next four days. Tany is the epitome of the stereotypical California girl, attractive, perky, and well—how do I say this?—well built. Her enthusiasm is contagious and comforting because we don't have to go at Hollywood alone.

It is fun to let our hair down and have drinks and good food and enjoy each other's company. Even the Fox crew joins us at dinner, but this time there are no cameras or reporters' questions. Quentin sits at the table too, as if sitting at a table is what all dogs do.

Finally, we hit the hotel and our beds. Morning will bring a full day of filming and preparing for the Guardian Awards ceremony. All of us are pooped—even Quent can't wait to climb into bed. He springs into bed with me, and off we go into slumberland. Quentin is undoubtedly dreaming of turkey sandwiches.

Morning arrives quickly. We have to get ready straightaway to film what in the media world is called a "walk and talk." All that really means is that I walk and talk while Quent walks with me. The setting couldn't be any more appealing—the Santa Monica boardwalk and the beaches of the Pacific Ocean.

We all walk and talk about the miracle, the plight of so many unwanted dogs, and about the upcoming awards. Schankman continues to mention the ceremony, and each time he does, my anxiety cranks up another notch. Quent chases pigeons and has a great time. Even Paul brought a tuxedo for the festivities.

Prom day was a cakewalk compared to what it's like for me to put on the first good suit I ever owned. But I do love to watch my Mom and my friends turn into prom queens. My friend Nicki Sanders arrives. She's funny as hell; I relax and everyone has a good laugh.

My mom needs some type of makeup thingy, and Nicki accommodates by pulling out a giant suitcase full of makeup and skin care products. I am awed by the display of beauty products. Quentin is transfixed. He steals a makeup pad and makes off with it. None of us stops him. He's probably bored watching everyone primp.

Dressed to the nines and ready to roll, Quentin and his "people" pull up to the swank hotel. Quentin is excited, as if he knows he is about to be showered with attention or turkey sandwiches. I, on the other hand, don sunglasses—not to be Joe Hollywood, but to put up an imaginary safety barrier to ward off a panic attack. Garlic and a cross would probably work just as well. It is hard to fathom that this special day is even here; maybe we all are still asleep.

Randy, Quentin, Pierce Brosnan, Dr. Goodall, and Dr. Katz of In Defense of Animals at the Hollywood gala.

Photo by Kelly Brinkman.

Feeling somewhat out of place, we all join the red carpet caravan alongside 007 himself, Pierce Brosnan. *This has to be a surreal dream.*

Everyone enthusiastically greets Quentin, and before I can take in my surroundings, we both are transported to the scariest room on the planet—the media room. It is jampacked with reporters and crews from national television shows. Cameras flash continuously. Quentin stands there perfectly as we pose with one celebrity after another. I love that he is a ham.

Finally I get to meet the one person I have idolized and who has inspired me for many years, Dr. Jane Goodall. But, like my first meeting with Quent, it is hindered by the glare of camera lights and reporters. Not private. Quentin immediately is smitten with Goodall, and she with him. She radiates compassion, kindness, empathy . . . and modesty. Quentin and I know we are in the presence of a special human being. She shows no signs of perspiration under the heat of all the lights. Quentin and Jane seem to belong together. Both possess this preternatural poise and sense of self. Each oddly embodies what is good in this world. It is hard to explain. Maybe these things are unexplainable.

Quentin and Dr. Goodall pose for the paparazzi.

It's interview after interview and Quent's story is hitting home. Thank God there is a special little blue drink that tastes like Kool-Aid being passed around. I grab one. Quent of course lives in the moment. I want to be him so badly. The sunglasses don't work.

The awards ceremony starts: It's the animal Emmys. Guests are doling out bites of vegan gourmet dinners to the ever-ready Quent. Who knew he liked eggplant?

Quent and I sit next to Steve Valentine of the television show *Crossing Jordan*. Steve will present the award to Quent and me. Boy, that sounds so Hollywood! But Steve is down to earth, a real animal lover, and caring, as is his wife. And she is empathetic, taking me out for a quick cigarette and Quent a pee break whenever she senses my panic.

The short film about my rescue work and Quentin's plight shows on the oversized screen for all 200 guests. The audience watches. I busily down one more pretty blue drink. Steve Valentine then announces Quentin, the "miracle dog," and me as award recipients. With shaky knees and about to vomit, I take Quentin and we ascend onto the stage.

I can't see the audience because of the lights and am grateful for that. Quent is next to me. I stand there thinking how Quent has affected so many people already and how he is making the world a better place for all animals. How to speak to such an audience? From the heart. The words finally come out of my mouth—simple words of wanting to see the end of the senseless killing of animals and what Quentin stands for. He is a messenger of hope.

I want to freeze this moment in time, for it is the first time I ever felt a part of something bigger than the world I live in back home. I want to freeze this moment and enjoy the applause Quentin is getting for being a survivor. They are applauding for *my* kid. For one brief moment, the hell in which so many animals live and die is center stage, and reform is getting tangible, room-shaking support. The heart of every person in that room is with Quentin, and all the Quentins who don't live to accept a Guardian Award. This means *hope*. But time—even at a moment like this—doesn't stand still. The beautiful Guardian Award, a painting of animals by world-renowned artist Linda Fisher, is presented. Quentin and I leave the stage. We both know that with this award comes a responsibility: to spread the message of the plight of all homeless animals. We both, for the rest of our respective lives, have that mission, and I will never forget the message of hope and love and support of that night.

The following day Tany picks Quent and me up to shuttle us to Hollywood for a meeting, a possible television show of our own with Film Garden Entertainment. The meeting goes fine. Quent sits on the sofa—he's in his Donald Trump mode. The program will be about what I do every day— rescuing dying dogs off the streets—but with a camera rolling and in different cities around the country. Everyone will see how these dogs live, how cruel people can be, and how wonderful these animals are. With Quent by my side, I am ready to sign on the dotted line.

Photo by Debbie Grim.

One tired Dad and Quent fly home from the Guardian Awards.

Photo by Kelly Brinkman.

Quentin and Randy interviewing—Quent is a pro!

A national forum for abandoned animals is a dream come true. As of this writing, the show is in development for Animal Planet or National Geographic Channel.

It is time to leave the stars behind and head back to reality—to St. Louis and the real world where stray dogs continue to roam the streets. Benny, a gentle, sweet street dog who'd found a "good" home, was instead being beaten. His guardian was out of work and was taking it out on the dog. Benny is now safe with us. Then there is Rexx, a large dying Golden mix who needed to be rescued as starvation and infection contaminated his system like cancer. There is work to do and there are lives on the line.

How do I end this book? How do I wrap up a story that is ongoing? I can't. I can tell you that, despite it all, I have high hopes. Quentin touches my life in many ways. He makes me a better human, a better guardian. I hope he has touched your souls, too. I hope he and millions of dogs like him, alone, left for dead, are now in your hearts. I hope there will be compassion in a world that seems to forget to protect the innocent. And I hope that if these animals are in your hearts, you will act.

Sadly, Candyman died two days before going to his forever home. He succumbed to old gunshot wounds and from respiratory difficulties as a result of smoke inhalation from his heroic deed.

Quentin's campaign to "Adapt and Save a Life."

Petey, my four-pound, twenty-year-old best friend, also passed away. His passing left me deeply depressed, and Quentin never left my side. He felt my pain and made it his. An eight-pounder with pneumonia and bad legs currently is in a papoose around my neck as I type. I named him Itchi. He isn't a replacement for Petey, but I think Petey is his guardian angel. The pack treats him just like they treated Pete. Bear, Petey's favorite, loves Itchi to death. The clan is back up to five.

The Guardian campaign has kicked off in St. Louis. The Adopt and Save a Life poster that features Quent now is on every metro bus, sending this important message loud and clear. Soon the poster will be plastered all over the New York transit system. That means another trip to launch the campaign there. Quent is ready.

Quentin has in fact returned to the Gasconade facility—the scene of the crime—but this time to assist in an adopt-a-thon. My fear that it might freak him out dissipated as soon as I saw him happily greet people as they entered the pound to adopt. It was the single most successful adoption event in the pound's sixty-two-year history. What a difference love and kindness make in this world! We left that day with a smile, knowing the shelter now had many empty cages and the gas chamber would get a rest.

It's not over for Quentin, though. He has a job to do. With me by his side, maybe one day we will see the end of gas chambers and the unnecessary killing of animals. A dog, and a Man Who Talks to Dogs, can dream.

Epilogue

ON MONDAY, AUGUST 9, 2004, THE CITY OF ST. LOUIS took the leap of faith and joined twelve American cities, one county, and one state in passing an ordinance to recognize individuals as the "guardian" of their animal companions, rather than simply "owner." Almost three million Americans now officially are recognized as animal guardians.

The effort to change St. Louis's language was spearheaded by my Energizer Bunny spokesdog, Quentin. It was an amazing victory. We celebrated by drinking—champagne for Dad and Quent's version of champagne, toilet water. This victory, however, was eclipsed by what took place the same week—Quentin's final exoneration—with the announcement of the end of the gas chamber by Mayor Francis Slay.

"I've been very concerned about the inhumane way that the city was euthanizing animals," Slay said. "Once I was down there and looked at it, we figured we had to find a way to change it."

Replacing the gas chamber with injections, he said, is "the right thing to do." [1]

Two paws up for the Mayor! I guess I had pegged him all wrong, and I am very proud of him and our city!

Photo by Bill Shelton.

The check that helped get rid of the gas chamber for good! Signed by Quentin.

St. Louis Mayor Francis Slay, Quent,
and Randy at City Hall.

I turn and glance at my four-
legged chum as I read about his latest
achievement and, as if on cue, he leaps
onto my lap and plants a very deliberate victory kiss. He knows we did
something enormous. I know there is
plenty more to do, but I make sure we
both bask in the recent triumphs with
more champagne and toilet water.

Photo by Jenn Foster.

Writing this book was an interesting experience for me. I had to juggle my
emotions, cry a bit, and think a lot. Quentin's tale isn't just one of survival,
although that is very cool and miraculous. His story is much larger than that and
is with me every day.

While writing this epilogue, I received an e-mail about a former shelter dog.
The dog had been hit by a car and had just three legs, but still had been success-
fully adopted (I thought). This type of e-mail is all too common:

I'm writing to see if you can help with Macy (formerly Missy). I got her from you almost
three years ago. In January I got married and moved from the two-family building I lived
in. The woman who lives on the second floor kept her for me because I couldn't take
her with me. She is now calling to say she can't keep her because she barks so much—
especially whenever someone visits.
Is it possible for you or someone in Stray Rescue to try and place her again? We're not
sure what to do about this.

This was my response to her:

Hi—Randy here, head of Stray Rescue. I can't lie and say I'm not disappointed, because
all dogs deserve to be cared for and taken full responsibility for, especially after adopting

her three years ago. We are their guardians and should show them as much compassion as possible. Marriage should not be used as an excuse to back out of your responsibility to Macy. Your application said marriage would not affect the dog's life. Had I known you'd change your mind, I would not have adopted her to you. With that said, let's at least be fair to Macy and try all avenues to avoid traumatizing her further. Barking can be controlled. They make no-bark collars specifically for this problem. Also, let's get the behaviorist, Dorene, involved as well. You owe it to Macy to try some steps here before we put her behind bars at the shelter. If this is not acceptable, please advise so we can make space for her at the shelter. Finding space is an enormous task in itself because there are so many homeless dogs who need our help.

Regards—

She said "no," but offered a big check to relieve her guilt.

Well, Macy returned to the shelter, back behind bars after three years. I remember her well, particularly her courage after losing a leg. When we adopted her out, her new guardian answered all the questions correctly—she said that even marriage or a move would not affect her love and ability to care for Macy. Did she lie?

I hope this woman reads this book. Maybe if she understood the scope of the problem and the fate that most homeless dogs face she would have tried harder. Maybe she will see that Quentin's courage and perseverance are qualities all humans should strive to attain. Maybe she'll learn about dogs' uncanny ability to love unconditionally, be loyal, make their guardians laugh, and provide comfort and companionship. Maybe she will "get it." Maybe.

No more *maybes*. Sorry, Macy. I lied to her when I whispered in her ear the day I rescued her, as she fearfully trembled in my arms, that her bad days were finally over.

Quentin lived to tell his story. He lived to change the mindset of basically good people who have forgotten or never grasped the fundamental emotion of compassion. In terms of character, if we all strived to be like our dogs, the world would be a much better place.

The Macys, the Candymans, the Quentins all have a message: Stop the killing, stop being selfish. Human beings created this horrendous problem that impacts so many innocent creatures, and it is up to all of us to come up with solutions. We owe it to them. We owe it to Quentin to restore his faith in humankind.

Photo by Randall Solomon.

Quentin

NOTES

Chapter One

[1] Dr. Elliot Katz, President–In Defense of Animals, private communication with author.

[2] Critter Haven, Inc., "Pet Overpopulation Epidemic." Retrieved October 9, 2004, www.critterhaven.org/images/Pet_Overpopulation.pdf

[3] Ibid.

[4] American Humane Association, "Animal Shelter Euthanasia." Retrieved October 9, 2004, www.americanhumane.org/site/PageServer?pagename=nr_fact_sheets_animal_euthanasia

[5] Ibid.

[6] Critter Haven, Inc., "Pet Overpopulation Epidemic." Retrieved October 9, 2004, www.critterhaven.org/images/Pet_Overpopulation.pdf

[7] Pawprints & Purrs, Inc., "Stop—Don't Litter! Spay and Neuter." Retrieved October 9, 2004, www.sniksnak.com/stop_s-n.html

[8] Elizabeth Forel, "Spay/Neuter Fact Sheet." March 1999. Shelter Reform Action Committee. Retrieved October 9, 2004, www.shelterreform.org/SpayFact.html

[9] Best Friends Animal Sanctuary, "No More Homeless Pets: New Hampshire Program Summary." Retrieved October 5, 2004, www.bestfriends.org.nomorehomelesspets/localnmhpprograms/nhstats.cfm

Chapter Two

[1] American Society for the Protection of Cruelty to Animals. Cited by SUN Network in "Shelter Statistics and Facts." Retrieved October 28, 2004, www.geocities.com/s_u_n_pa/ShelterFacts.html

[2] Ibid.

[3] *The Worcester Telegram*, West Gardner, February 6, 2001; *The Boston Herald*, February 7 and 13, 2001; The Associated Press, February 12, 2001. Pet-Abuse.Com, "Deplorable Conditions at City Animal Shelter." Retrieved October 28, 2004, http://pet-abuse.com/cases/154/MA/US/1

[4] Carmel Cafiero, "Questionable Euthanasia Practices at County Animal Shelter," December 2, 2003. WSVN-TV FOX Miami. Retrieved November 4, 2004, www.wsvn.com/features/articles/carmelcase/c21

[5] Ibid.

Chapter Three

[1] Bill Baskerville, "Many Abandoned Animals Die in Taxpayer-Funded Gas Chambers," Associated Press. Originally published in *The Daily Press*, Richmond, Virginia, June 16, 2002.

[2] Faith Maloney, Animal Care Director–Best Friends Animal Sanctuary, personal communication with author.

[3] American Veterinary Medical Association, "2000 Report of the AVMA Panel on Euthanasia," *JAVMA*, Vol. 218, No. 5, March 1, 2001, p. 679. Retrieved October 28, 2004, www.avma.org/resources/euthanasia.pdf

[4] Ibid.

[5] The Humane Society of the United States, "General Statement Regarding Euthanasia Methods for Dogs And Cats," 1999. Retrieved November 8, 2004, http://files.hsus.org/web-files/HSI/E_Library_PDFs/eng_euth_statement.pdf

[6] Ibid.

[7] American Humane Association, *Operational Guide for Animal Care and Control Agencies*, and Humane Society of the United States. Cited in "Yadkin County, North Carolina, Update: Animals Continue to Suffer," by People for the Ethical Treatment of Animals. Retrieved November 8, 2004, www.peta.org/feat/yadkin/co2.html

[8] People for the Ethical Treatment of Animals, "Yadkin County, North Carolina, Update: Animals Continue to Suffer." Retrieved November 8, 2004, www.peta.org/feat/yadkin/co2.html

Chapter Four

[1] Maryann Mott, "U.S. Facing Feral Dog Crisis." August 21, 2003. *National Geographic News.* Retrieved November 8, 2004, http://news.nationalgeographic.com/news/2003/08/0821_030821_straydogs.html

[2] National Broadcasting Co., Inc. NBC News Transcripts, *The Today Show,* August 9, 2003

[3] Joseph Spohn, interview with author, December 2003.

[4] Sarah Casey Newman, interview with author, December 2003.

Chapter Seven

[1] Lori Golden, "Randy Grim—Creating Awareness that ALL Animals Should Be Cared for and Guarded from Harm's Way." *The Pet Press*, August 1999. Retrieved October 28, www.thepetpress-la.com/articles/randygrim/htm

Chapter Nine

[1] RedNova, "Dog Survives Euthanization," December 20, 2003. Retrieved November 8, 2004, www.rednova.com/news/stories/5/2003/12/20/story104.html

[2] Ed Bok, private communication with author.

[3] Maddie's Fund, "Defining No Kill." Retrieved November 11, 2001, http://www.maddiesfund.org/nokill/nokill_define_what.html

[4] Best Friends Animal Sanctuary, "Annual Report for 2003." Retrieved November 11, 2004, www.bestfriends.org/aboutus/annualreport03.cfm

[5] Merrit Clifton, private communication with author.

Epilogue

[1] Michael Sorkin, "Slay Plans to Get Rid of Gas Chamber at Pound." *St. Louis Post-Dispatch*, August 14, 2004.

APPENDIX A
RESOURCES

Stray Rescue of St. Louis
> http://www.strayrescue.org

In Defense of Animals
> http://www.idausa.org

Links to Animal Shelters, Rescue Organizations, Spay/Neuter Programs, etc.
> http://www.saveourstrays.com/links.htm

Hearts United for Animals (National No Kill Shelter, Sanctuary and Animal Welfare Organization)
> http://www.hua.org/

Kyler Laird's Animal Rescue Resources (website that lists animal welfare and no-kill organizations in the U.S. and around the world)
> http://www.ecn.purdue.edu/~laird/animal_rescue/

Pets 911 (website that searches for no-kill shelters in your area based on your zip code)
> http://www.1888pets911.org/animal_shelters.html

Website for no-kill shelters in British Columbia, Canada
> http://dmoz.org/Society/Organizations/Animal_Welfare/Rescues_and_
> Shelters/Regional/North_America/Canada/British_Columbia/

Websites for no-kill shelters in the U.S. by state as well as in foreign countries
> http://www.sheltersearch.net/shelters/inmain.html
> http://www.greenpeople.org/humanesociety.htm

APPENDIX B
NO-KILL ORGANIZATIONS (by no means a complete list)

Alabama

Anelia Animal Sanctuary—Oneonta
PAWS (Pets are Worth Saving)—Huntsville
Rescue & Adoption—Huntsville
Save the Animals—Rainbow City
Saving Animals from Euthanasia—Florala
Scottish Terrier Rescue of North Alabama—Decatur
Scottish Terrier Rescue Network—Birmingham
The Ark, Inc.—Toney
West Alabama Animal Rescue—Tuscaloosa

Alaska

Adopt-A-Cat—Anchorage
Alaska Humane Society—Anchorage

Arizona

A to Z Rescue—Phoenix
Arizona Animal & Wildlife League of the White Mountains—Show Low
Aid for Stray Cats and Canines—Phoenix
Animal League of Green Valley—Green Valley
Animals Benefit Club of Arizona—Phoenix
Arizona Cat Assistance Team—Phoenix
Arizona Feline Network—Scottsdale
Arizona Homeless Animals Rescue Team—Glendale
Cat Help & Rescue Movement—Phoenix
CHARM—Phoenix
Citizens for North Phoenix Strays—Phoenix
Citizens for Scottsdale Strays—Scottsdale
Coalition of All-Breed Rescue—Phoenix
Foundation for Animals in Risk (FAIR)—Tucson
Foothills Animal Rescue—Cave Creek
Friends of Alley Cats of Tucson (FACT)—Tucson
Friends for Life Animal Sanctuary—Gilbert
Hacienda de los Milagros—Chino Valley
HELP—Help Elevate Life for Pets—Phoenix
Hermitage No-Kill Cat Shelter—Tucson
Noah's Animal Rescue—Phoenix
Paw Placement—Scottsdale
Pets on Wheels of Scottsdale, Inc.—Scottsdale
Protect Animals through Angels, Inc.—Scottsdale
R.E.S.C.U.E.—Phoenix
Sun Cities Animal Rescue—Sun City

Arkansas
    Floppy Dog House Basset Rescue—Blytheville
    For the Sake of the Animals—Mena
    Friends of the Animals—Bella Vista
    Garland County Animal Welfare—Hot Springs
    Grant Count Animal Protection Society, Inc.—Prattsville
    Humane Society of Clark County—Arkadelphia
    Humane Society of Pulaski County—Little Rock

California
    10th Life Foundation—Santa Barbara
    Alpha Canine Sanctuary—Bakersfield
    Angel Puss & Pooch Rescue—West Hills
    Animal Abuse Prevention Agency—Huntington Beach
    Animal Assistance League of Orange County—Midway City
    Animal Helpline—Morongo Valley
    Animal Outreach—Diamond Springs
    Animal Rescue of Fresno—Fresno
    Animal Rescue Coalition—Arroyo Grande
    Animal Samaritans S.P.C.A.—Thousand Palms
    Animal Shelter Assistance Program (ASAP)—Santa Barbara
    Animals at Risk Care Sanctuary—Modesto
    Asians for Humans, Animals and Nature—San Francisco
    Beagles and Buddies—El Monte
    Benevolent Animal Rescue Committee (BARC)—Temecula
    Benicia-Vallejo Humane Society—Vallejo
    Berkeley East Bay Humane Society—Berkeley
    Blue Bell Foundation—Laguna Beach
    BroDoFed Sanctuary International—Garberville
    California Feline Foundation—Fresno
    C.A.R.E.—Campbell
    Cat Crossing—Encino/Santa Monica
    Catalina Island Cats— Catalina Island
    Cats About Town Society—Orangevale
    Cats Allied Tactical Support—Morongo Valley
    Cats in Need of Humane Care—Pomona
    Coastal Animal Service Authority—San Clemente
    Community of Compassion for Animals—Orland
    Companion Pet Retreat—Mission Viejo
    Delta Humane Society—Stockton
    DELTA Rescue—Glendale
    East Bay Animal Referral—Oakland
    FAIRE—Santa Rosa
    Feral Cat Coalition—San Diego
    Forgotten Felines of Sonoma County—Santa Rosa
    Foundation for Care of Indigent Animals—Spring Valley
    Friends for Pets Foundation—Sun Valley

The Friends of Animals Foundation—Los Angeles
Friends of Cats—El Cajon
Friends of the Fairmont Animal Shelter—San Leandro
Greyfoot Rescue—Ventura
Greyhound Protection League—Penn Valley
Happy Tails Pet Sanctuary—Sacramento
HART Muttmatchers—Fillmore
Hayward Animal Shelter—Hayward
Helen Woodward Animal Center—Rancho Santa Fe
Homeless Animal Rescue Team—Cambria
Homeless Cat Network—San Carlos
Humane Animal Rescue Team—Cambria
Humane Society of Sonoma County—Santa Rosa
Humane Society of the Desert /Orphan Pet Oasis—North Palm Springs
Kitten Rescue—Los Angeles
Lange Foundation—Los Angeles
LIFE Animal Rescue—Agoura
Life Line Cat Rescue—Ben Lomond
Living Free—Mountain Center
Millerwood Animal Rescue & Sanctuary—Burbank
Milo Foundation—Willits
New Lease On Life Animal Rescue—Los Angeles
Noah's Bark Pet Rescue—Los Angeles
North Bay Canine Rescue & Placement—Petaluma
North County Humane Society—Atascadero
Not So Purrrfect Angels Cat Sanctuary/Retirement Home—Fresno
PAL Rescue & Adoption—Gardena
Pampered Paws Pet Services—Redondo Beach
People & Cats Together—Los Angeles
Pet Adoption Fund—Canoga Park
Pet Animal Foundation—Hesperia
Pet Finders—Sacramento
Pet Friends—Hollister
Pet Network—Saratoga
Pet Orphans Fund—Los Angeles
Pet Pride—Los Angeles
Pet Pro Life Adoption & Placement, Inc.—Orange County
Pet Rescue of Unwanted Dogs—Kingsbury
Pets in Need—Redwood City
Pets Lifeline—Sonoma
Project Purr—Santa Cruz
PURRS—Oakland
Purple Cow Animal Shelter—Los Angeles
Redlands Humane Society—Redlands
Riverside Humane Society—Riverside
San Francisco SPCA—San Francisco
Save A Pet, Inc.—Desert Hot Springs

Seal Beach Animal Care Center—Seal Beach
Second Chance Animal Rescue—San Juan Bautista
Second Chance at Love Humane Society—Templeton
Shelter Dog Rescue Project at US Davis—Davis
Solano County Friends of Animals—Vallejo
South County Humane Society—Arroyo Grande
The Senior Dogs Project—San Francisco
Town and Country Humane Society—Orland
Tri-Valley Animal Rescue—Pleasanton
Tony LaRussa Animal Rescue Foundation—Walnut Creek
Valley Humane Society—Pleasanton
We Care Animal Society—St. Helena
Yolo County SPCA—Davis

Colorado
Animal Orphanage—Denver
Animal Rescue & Adoption Society—Denver
Boulder County Humane Society—Boulder
Cat Care Society—Lakewood
Colorado Animal Welfare & Protection Society—Pueblo
Colorado Greyhound Adoptions—Denver
Denver Animal Foundation—Glendale
Doghouse Animal Sanctuary—Durango
Dreampower Animal Rescue Foundation—Colorado Springs
Every Creature Counts—Lyons
Friends of Park County Animals—Bailey
Fur Purries—Pueblo
Lifeline Puppy Rescue—Henderson
MaxFund Animal Adoption Center—Denver
Mile Hi Humane Society—Thornton
Pitkin Animal Welfare Society—Aspen
Safe Haven Foundation—Aurora

Connecticut
Aid to Helpless Animals, Inc.—Bloomfield
Animals Friends of Connecticut—West Hartford
Animal Welfare Society—New Milford
Animal Welfare and Rights Entity—Tolland
Cat Calls—West Hartford
Catales, Inc.—Middletown
Connecticut Cat Rescue Web—New Haven
Forgotten Feline—Clintons
Greater New Haven Cat Project—New Haven
Hope Alliance Adoption Center—Guilford
I'm Homeward Bound—Colchester
Kitty Angels—Tolland
Last Post—Falls Village

Meow Meow, Inc.—Litchfield
New Leash on Life—Fairfield/New Haven

Delaware

Animal Humane Sanctuary—Smyrna
Delaware Humane Association—Wilmington
Paws for Life—Middletown

Florida

Abandoned Pet Rescue—Fort Lauderdale
Adopt-A-Pet—Miami
Alliance for Animals—Orlando
Animal Refuge Center—Fort Meyers
Animal Rescue Foundation—Longwood
Animal Rescue Movement—Jacksonville
Animal Shelter Fund—Boca Raton
Bear Foundation—Pointe Verda Beach
Brevard Pet Adoption Center—Melbourne
Cats in the Cradle—Lake Park
Cat Network—Miami
Cat Woman's Shelter, Inc.—Sarasota
Englewood Animal Rescue Sanctuary—Englewood
Florida Dog Adoption Center—Attamonte Springs
Give Them A Second Chance—Plantation
Humane Society of Hernando County—Brooksville
Humane Society of Pensacola— Pensacola
Humane Society of Pinellas—Clearwater
Leesburg Humane Society—Leesburg
Levy County Humane Society—Willison
Miami-Dade Police Dept. Animal Services Unit—Miami
Pet Action League—Debary
Pet Rescue by Judy—Orlando
Pet Rescue—Miami
Pet Welfare—Elgin AFB
Save Our Cats & Kittens (SOCKS)—Ft. Walton Beach
Shawn-n-Jen's Animal Connection, Inc.—Lighthouse Point
SPCA of Central Florida—Orlando, Sanford
South Lake Animal League—Clermont
St. Francis Animal Rescue of Venice—Venice
St. Francis Society Animal Rescue—Tampa Bay
The Hernando Humane Society—Brooksville
Volunteer Service for Animals—Naples

Georgia

All Creatures Are Truly Special—Dahlonega
Animal Welfare and Rescue Effort of Savannah—Savannah

Atlanta Area Rescue List—http://spotsociety.org/atl_shelter_list.htm
CSRA Humane Society—Augusta
DeKalb Humane Society—Decatur
DogPak Rescue—Rome
Good Mews Animal Foundation—Marietta
Homeless Animal Rescue and Placement Services Inc. (HARPS)—Macon
Lake Park Area Animal Rescue—Lake Park
Paulding Volunteer Animal Rescue—Powder Springs
Pet Orphans—Atlanta
Pets are Worth Saving (PAWS)—Coastal Empire
RescueCats, Inc.—Fayetteville
Save-a-Life Animal Welfare Organization—Savannah
Society of Humane Friends—Lawrenceville
Southern Hope—Atlanta

Hawaii

9th Life Hawaii—Makawao
East Maui Animal Refuge—Haiku
Feline Foundation of Maui—Puunene
Hawaii Cat Foundation—Honolulu
Hawaii Animal Sanctuary— Honolulu

Idaho

Just Strays Animal Foundation—Boise
Pets Are Worth Saving (PAWS) for Life—Boise

Illinois

ADOPT Animals Deserving of Proper Treatment—Naperville
Adopt-A-Pet—Benld
Animal Adoption Associates—Chicago
Animal Care League (ACL)—Oak Park
Animal Protective Association—Chicago
Animal Protective League (Waggin Tales)—Springfield
Assisi Animal Foundation—Crystal Lake
Association for the Protection of Animals—Granite City
Bark—Bringing Aid to Rescued K-9's—Skokie
Cat Guardians, Inc.—Lombard
Central Illinois Sheltie Rescue—Bloomington
Community Animal Rescue Effort—Evanston
DeKalb County Humane Society—Genoa
Felines, Inc.—Chicago
The Furry Friends Foundation—Chicago
Harmony House for Cats—Chicago
Homes for Endangered and Lost Pets (HELP)—St. Charles
Humane Society of Rock Island County—Milan
Illinois Alaskan Malamute Rescue Association—Mt. Prospect
Kindness, Inc.—Elgin

Lake Shore Animal Shelter—Chicago
Noah's Ark Animal Sanctuary—Rockford
Pet Outreach—Peoria
Pet Project, Inc.—Grand Ridge
Pet Rescue—Bloomingdale
Pets in Need—Ringwood
Project Hope Humane Society—Metropolis
Quad City Animal Welfare Center—Milan
Recycling Animals in Need (RAIN)—Hinckley
Save-a-Pet, Inc.—Grayslake
Second Chance Pet Adoption Organization—Elk Grove Village
Society of St. Francis—Wadsworth
Strays Halfway House—Schaumberg
Tazewell Animal Protective Society—Pekin
Tree House Animal Foundation—Chicago
Tri-County Animal Protection League—Dixon
West Suburban Humane Society—Downers Grove
Will County Humane Society—Shorewood

Indiana

Animal Welfare League of Kosciusko County—Warsaw
Cats Haven—Indianapolis
Dubois County Humane Society—Jasper
Fried's Cat Shelter—Michigan City
Harmony Haven Animal Sanctuary—Terre Haute
Home for Friendless Animals—Hamilton County
Independent Cat Society, Inc.—Westville
NOAH—Hammond
Pet Refuge, Inc.—South Bend
Second Chance—Boone County
Strays in the Garden—Hessville

Iowa

Animal Lifeline of Iowa—Carlisle
C and W Rustic Hollow Shelter—Nashua
Noah's Ark Animal Foundation—Fairfield
Protectors of Animal Welfare—Fort Madison

Kansas

The Cat Association of Topeka (CAT)—Topeka

Kentucky

Animal Refuge Center—Vine Grove
The Ark Project—Frankfort
Home at Last Animal Sanctuary—SalvisaPet Lovers United—Madisonville
The Shamrock foundation—Louisville
The Trixie Foundation—Webbville

Louisiana
>   Arklatex Dog/Cat Adopt and Friends—Haughton
>   Bell Animal Shelter—Lake Charles
>   Humane Society Adoption Center—Monroe
>   Lafayette Animal Aid—Lafayette
>   St. John Humane Society—La Place

Maine
>   Ark Animal Shelter—Cherryfield
>   Boothbay Region Humane Society/Lincoln County Animal Shelter—
>   Boothbay Harbor
>   Camden-Rockport Animal Rescue League—Rockport
>   Hemlock Hill Farm Sanctuary—North Lebanon
>   Humane Society of Knox County—Rockland
>   Marlee Animal Rescue Shelter—Wells
>   Peaceable Kingdom—Brooks
>   Protectors of Animal Life Society—East Winthrop

Maryland
>   Action Pet Rescue Service—Baltimore
>   Alley Cat Rescue—Mount Rainier
>   Animal Rescue—Baltimore
>   Cat & Kitten Rescue of Baltimore—Baltimore
>   Catwoman Rescue and Adoption—Hampstead
>   Defenders of Animal Rights—Phoenix
>   Heavens Gate Animal Rescue—Baltimore
>   Lucky Ones—Charlotte Hall
>   Montgomery County SPCA—Gaithersburg
>   Partnership for Animal Welfare (PAW)—Greenbelt
>   Patuxent Animal Welfare Society—Lusby
>   Potomac Stray Cat Rescue, Inc.—Rohrersville

Massachusetts
>   Alliance for Animals—Boston
>   Animal Advocates—North Dartmouth
>   Animal Shelter, Inc.—Sterling
>   Animal Umbrella, Inc.—Lynn
>   Baypath Humane Society of Hopkinton—Hopkinton
>   Bosler Humane Society—Templeton
>   Buddy Dog Humane Society—Sudbury
>   Cape Ann Animal Aid Association—Gloucester
>   Carver Cat Shelter—Carver
>   Cattrap, Inc.—West Tisbury
>   Cavy Rescue—South Boston
>   Ce-Ce & Friends Humane Society—Quincey
>   Champs Mini Shelter—Wareham
>   Commonwealth Cares Humane Society—Cohasette

Eleanor Sonsini Municipal Animal Shelter—Pittsfield
Ellen M. Gifford Sheltering Home—Brighton
F.A.C.E.S. Dog Rescue—West Springfield
Greyhound Rescue of N.E., Inc.—Mendon
Habitat for Cats—North Dartmouth
Homeward Hound Humane Society—Brockton
Jeff's Companion Animal Shelter—Westport
Just Cats, Inc.—Mansfield
Kitty Angels—Tyngsboro
Kitty Love Cat Shelter—Wilmington
Last Chance Feral Rescue—North Dartmouth
Last Resort—Hanover
Medfield Animal Shelter—Medfield
Melrose Humane Society—Melrose
Merrimack River Feline Rescue—Salisbury
Milford Humane Society—Milford
Milton Animal League—Milton
Neponset Valley Humane Society—Canton
North Attleborough Animal Shelter—North Attleborough
North Shore Feline Rescue—Middleton
Northeast Animal Shelter—Salem
Pat Brody Shelter for Cats—Lunenburg
PawSafe Animal Rescue—Medford
Pet Adoption & Welfare Services—Edgartown
PoundHounds—Hopkinton
Pookie's Pals—Norwell
Purr-Fect Cat Shelter—Medway
Standish Humane Society—Duxbury
Strays in Need—Danvers
Volunteer Humane Society—Lancaster
Yankee Golden Retriever Rescue—Hudson

Michigan

Adopt-a-Pet Rescue—Allegan
Adopt-a-Pet, Inc.—Fenton
All Paws Animal Rescue—Ann Arbor
Animals Deserve Adequate Protection Today and Tomorrow—Royal Oak
Animal Placement Bureau—Lansing
Animal Welfare Society of Southeastern Michigan—Madison Heights
Betsy's Haven Rescue—Morley
Cat Connection—Berkeley
Charly's Exotic And Small Animal Rescue—Utica
Companion Cat Adoption Agency—Grand Blanc
GreyHeart Greyhound Rescue and Adoption of Michigan—Livonia
Help Orphaned Pets Everywhere—Ironwood
Humane Society of Saginaw—Saginaw
Jethro's Place Animal Sanctuary—Memphis

Kalamazoo Animal Rescue—Kalamazoo
K-9 Stray Rescue League—Oxford
Michigan Animal Adoption Network—Livonia
Michigan Animal Rescue League, Inc.—Pontiac
Mid Michigan Society for Animal Protection—Mason
Peninsula Animal Welfare Society, Inc. (PAWS)—Sault Ste. Marie
Pets Alive, Inc.—Cassopolis
Volunteers For Animals—Utica
West Michigan SPCA—Muskegon

Minnesota

Animal Ark—Twin Cities
Beltrami Humane Society—Bemidji
Contented Critters—Makinen
Feline Rescue, Inc.—St. Paul
Gemini Rottweiler & K-9 Sanctuary—Madison
Hearts United for Animals—Midwest Shelter
Humane Society of Polk County—Crookston
Lake Superior Humane Society—Knife River
Last Hope, Inc.—Farmington
Mower County Humane Society—Austin
Pet Haven, Inc. of Minnesota—Minneapolis
Rainbow Rescue—Prior Lake
Rescuers.org—Duluth
Second Chance Animal Rescue—White Bear Lake

Mississippi

Cedarhill Animal Sanctuary—Caledonia
IDA's Project Hope—Grenada

Missouri

Animal Haven—Kansas City
Castaway Animal Rescue Effort (CARE)—Verona
Cat Network—St. Louis
Feline Connection—Chesterfield
Happy Tails Animal Sanctuary—Columbia
Home for Endangered and Lost Pets (HELP) Inc.—Raymore
Humane Society of the Branson Tri-Lakes Area—Reeds Spring
Kansas City Pet Adoption League—Kansas City
M'shoogy's Animal Rescue—Savannah
Open Door Animal Sanctuary—St. Louis
Pet Search—Wildwood
Second Chance—Columbia
Society for the Treatment of Abandoned and Fractured Friends—Laurie
St. Charles Humane Society—St. Charles
Stray Rescue of St. Louis—St. Louis

Montana
>   Humane Society of Gallatin Valley—Bozeman
>   Last Chance Cat Sanctuary—Billings
>   Montana Large Animal Sanctuary & Rescue—Polson

Nebraska
>   Companion Animal Rescue Effort Society—Raymond
>   Hearts United for Animals—Auburn
>   Merlin's Refuge—Omaha
>   Midwest Animal Shelter—Auburn
>   Panhandle Humane Society—Scotsbluff

Nevada
>   Betty Honn's Animal Adoption, Ltd.—Henderson
>   F.L.O.C.K.—Las Vegas
>   Las Vegas Humane Society—Las Vegas
>   Media Partners for Pets—Las Vegas
>   Nevada SPCA—Las Vegas
>   Pets Bed N Breakfast—Las Vegas
>   Pet Network—Incline Village
>   ShelterDog Rescue—Las Vegas
>   Unicorn Point Animal Sanctuary—Winnemucca

New Hampshire
>   Above the Notch Humane Society—Littleton
>   Feline Friends Rescue/Adoption League—Salem
>   Greater Derry Humane Society—East Perry
>   Kitty Angels—Tyngsboro
>   Lakes Region Humane Society—Wolfboro
>   Lancaster Humane Society—Lancaster

New Jersey
>   American Society for the Welfare of Cats—Bellmawr
>   Animal Adoption Center—Lindenwood
>   Burlington County Animal Alliance—Mt. Holly
>   Cloister Animal Welfare Society—Cloister
>   Friends of Homeless Animals—Trenton
>   Humane Society of Bergen County—Lyndhurst
>   Humane Society of Ocean City—Ocean City
>   Hunterdon County SPCA—Milford
>   Jersey Animal Coalition, Inc.—Maplewood
>   Lindenwold Animal Adoption—Lindenwold
>   Little Egg Harbor Animal Rescue—Tuckerton
>   New Jersey Rescue, Transport and Foster—Keyport
>   Noah's Ark Animal Placement & Rescue—Clark
>   Open Your Heart—Belle Mead

Ramapo Bergen Animal Refuge—Oakland
Salem County Humane Society—Carney's Point

New Mexico

Albuquerque Cat Action Team (ACAT)— Albuquerque
Heart and Soul Animal Sanctuary—Santa Fe
New Mexico Animal Friends—Albuquerque
People's Anti-Cruelty Assoc./Albuquerque Animal Rescue— Albuquerque
Safe Haven Animal Sanctuary—Las Cruces

New York

A Cause for Paws—Manhattan
ACT—Queens
Ada Howe Kent Memorial Shelter—Calverton
Adirondack Save A Stray—Corinth
Animal Haven—Queens
Animal Lovers League Shelter—Albany
Animal Service League—Rochester
Bide-A-Wee Home Association—Manhattan
Bobbi and the Strays—Queens
Brooklyn Animal Resource Coalition (BARC)—Brooklyn
Citizens Committee for Animal Rights—Queens
City Critters—Manhattan
Elmsford Animal Shelter—Elmsford
Essie Dabrusin Cat Sanctuary—Beacon
Feline Rescue, Inc.—Staten Island
Fulton County SPCA—Broadalbin
Furever Animals, Inc.—Montgomery
Grateful Paw Cat Shelter—Huntington
Greece Residents Assisting Stray Pets (GRASP)—Rochester
Hamburg-Eden Animal Rescue Team—Hamburg
Jefferson County SPBA—Watertown
Kent Animal Shelter/Spay/Neuter Clinic—Calverton
Kings Highway Cat Rescue—Brooklyn
Kitty Corner—Liverpool
Kitty Kind—Manhattan
League for Animal Protection, Inc.—Lindenhurst
Little Orphan Animals—Peekskill
Little Shelter—Huntington
Mid Hudson Animal Aid—Beacon
Mighty Mutts—Brooklyn
New Yorkers for Companion Animals—Manhattan
North Fork Animal Welfare League—Southold
North Shore Animal League—Port Washington
Peace Plantation Animal Shelter—Walton
People Against Cruelty to Animals—Watertown
People for Animal Welfare Society (PAWS)—Albion

Pet Pride of New York—Victor
Pets Alive, Inc.—Middletown
Project PAW, Inc.—Binghamton
SAVE—Queens
Save Our Strays—Brooklyn
Sentient Creatures, Inc.—New York
Scottsville Veterinary Adoptions—Rochester
Scottsville Veterinary Adoptions—Scottsville
SPCA Allegany County—Wellsville
SPCA of Cattaraugus County—Olean
SPCA of Upstate NY—Queensbury
Tigger Foundation—Manhattan
Tri-State Animal Rescue Services, Inc.
The North Country SPCA—Hudson Falls
Westside Animal Rescue—New York
Whiskers Animal Benevolent League—Albany

North Carolina

All Creatures Great and Small—Hendersonville
Animal Compassion Network—Skyland
Animal Inn—Wilmington
Animal Rescue and Foster Program—Greensboro
Burke County Friends for Animals—Morganton
Catman-2, Inc.—Cashiers
Cumberland County Animal Haven—Fayetteville
Eutha-Not Animal Shelter, Inc.—Forest City
Forsyth Humane Society—Winston-Salem
Happy Hills Animal Foundation, Inc.—Staley
The Haven—Raeford
Henderson County Humane Society—Hendersonville
Humane Society of Charlotte—Charlotte
Humane Society of Jackson County—Sylva
Humane Society of Randolph County—Asheboro
Independent Animal Rescue—Hillsborough
Let's Go Home Now—Wake Forest
Paw's Place—Winnabow
Placing Animals Within Society (PAWS)—Bryson City
Pitt County Humane Society—Greenville
Project HALO (Helping Animals Live On)—Charlotte
S.A.F.E. Haven for Cats—Raleigh
Second Chance Pet Adoptions—Cary
Snowflake Animal Rescue—Raleigh
Southport/Oak Island Animal Rescue—Southport
Haven, Friends for Life—Raeford

North Dakota

Central Dakota Humane Society—Mandan

Ohio

Angel Animal Rescue—Middletown
Angels for Animals—Canfield
Bide-A-Wee Cat Shelter—North Royalton
Bosney-Densmore Animal Shelter—Mingo Junction
Caroline's Kids Pet Rescue—Mayfield
Cat Welfare Association—Columbus
Cats Are People Too—Warren
Erie Shores Humane Society—Elyria
Evergreen-Doe Humane Society—Dayton
Forgotten 4-Paws—Columbus
Friends For Life Animal Haven—Canal Winchester
Fulton County Humane Society—Delta
Geauga Humane Society—Chardon
Great Dane Rescue of Ohio—Beavercreek
Kitty Comfort—Hamilton
Lawrence County Humane Society Abuse and Adoption Center—Ironton
League for Animal Welfare—Batavia
Tri-County Animal Protective League—Akron
Wood County Humane Society—Bowling Green

Oklahoma

Almost Home Animal Rescue—Shawnee
Animal Rescue Foundation—Tulsa
Animal Rescue Foundation of Bartlesville—Bartlesville
Free To Live—Edmond
Homeward Bound Bryant County Humane Society—Bryant
HOPE of Texoma—Lexington
Last Chance for Life—Oklahoma City
Pets and People Humane Society—Oklahoma City
Ponca Animal Welfare Society—Ponca City
Promoting Animal Welfare Society, Inc.—Muskogee
SafeHaven Humane Society—Albany
Second Chance Animal Sanctuary—Norman
The Russell-Davis Animal Sanctuary—Tahlequah

Oregon

Animal Aid—Portland
Animal Rescue Foundation of Oregon—Fossil
Animal Rescue League of Central Oregon—Bend
Cat Adoption Team—Sherwood
Columbia Humane Society—St. Helens
Committed Alliance to Strays—Medford
Evergreen-Doe Humane Society—McMinnville
Florence Area Humane Society—Florence
Planned Pethood, Inc.—La Grande
Red Bear Sanctuary—Bandon

Rogue Valley Humane Society—Grants Pass
SafeHaven Humane Society—Albany
Southern Oregon Humane Society—Medford
Spay & Neuter Humane Association—Astoria
Unicorn Point Animal Sanctuary—Klamath Falls
Vets for Pets—Portland

Pennsylvania

Animal Angels—Connellsville
Animal Care Sanctuary—East Smithfield
Animal Friends—Pittsburgh
Animal Orphans, Inc.—Hatfield
Animal Protectors of Allegheny Valley—New Kensington
Animal Rescue Inc.—New Freedom
Animals in Distress—Allentown
Because You Care, Inc.—McKean
Cat Ladies, Inc.—Morton
Centre County PAWS—State College
CRP for Cats Society—Eagleville
Francisvale Home for Smaller Animals—Wayne
Good Mews—Trexlertown
Helen O. Krause Animal Foundation—Dillsburg
Hillside SPCA—Pottsville
Hope for the Animals—Morrisville
Kitty and K9 Connection—Drexeler Hill
Lifetime of Love No Kill Shelter for Cats—Riegelsville
Lycoming Animal Protection Society—Williamsport
Northampton-Boro Animal Shelter—Northampton
One By One Animal Rescue—Kutztown
Orphans of the Storm—Kittanning
Paws and Claws—Wellsboro
Peaceable Kingdom, Inc.—Allentown
Pet Adoption and Lifecare Society (PALS)—Springfield
Pet Connection—Avonmore
Preservation of Animal Welfare & Safety (PAWS)—Harrisburg
Philly Rescue—Philadelphia
Valley Cat Rescue—Wilkes-Barre

Rhode Island

Animal Rescue League of Southern Rhode Island—Peace Dale
Defenders of Animals—Providence
Volunteer Services for Animals—Providence
Hope for Animals—Slatersville
Volunteers for Animals—Block Island

South Carolina

Animal Protection League of South Carolina—Hopkins

Carolina Cats Adopt-A-Kitty—Columbia
Concerned Citizens for Animals—Simpsonville
Concerned Citizens for Animals—Spartanburg
Critter Connection—Spartanburg
Feline Refuge, Inc.—Mt. Pleasant
Have-a-Heart 2000—Columbia
Hilton Head Humane Association—Hilton Head Island
Humane Society of Greenwood—Greenwood
Pet Helpers—Charleston
Project Pet—Columbia
PurrFect Kitty Rescue Shelter—Cowpens
SPCA of Cumberland County—Fayetteville
Steve's Dog Shelter—Conway
True Ethics for Animals Rescue—Montmorenci

Tennessee

Angel Wings Cat Rescue—Kingston
Northeast Tennessee Animal League—Blountville

Texas

Adopt-A-Cat—Houston
Adopt-A-Pet—Victoria
Alley Cat Rescues—Manor
Animal Adoption Center—Garland
Animal Defense League of Texas—San Antonio
Animal Guardians of America—Plano
Animal Refuge Foundation—Sherman
Arlington Humane Society—Arlington
Campus Cat Coalition—Univ. of Texas—Austin
Central Texas SPCA Williamson County—Leander
Church of the Ark—Van Alstyne
City Animal Shelter—Austin
Clay County Animal Shelter—Henrietta
Coppell Humane Society—Coppell
Critter Buddies—Elgin
DFW Humane Society—Irving
Ellis County Volunteer Animal Shelter—Red Oak
Feral Cat Connection—Houston
Friends for Animals No Kill Adoption Shelter—Granbury
Fuzzy Face Pet Rescue—Fort Worth
Fuzzy Friends Rescue—Waco
Help for Helpless Animals—Dallas
Humane Animal Rescue Team—Irvine
German Shepherd Dog Rescue of Houston—Houston
Greyhound Friends of Texas—Garland
Greyhound Pets of America/Houston, Inc.—Houston
Humane Society of Aransas County—Fulton

Humane Society of Austin and Travis County—Austin
Humane Society of Dallas County—Dallas
Lexee's Legacy—Carrollton
Metroport Humane Society—Roanoke
Mid Cities Humane Society—Grand Prairie
Operation Kindness—Carrollton
PAWS—Lago Vista
Paws For Life—Christoval
Puppy Love Rescue—Austin
Safe Haven Animal Shelter—Millsap
Sanctuary for Unwanted Animals and Care—Brookshire
Save Pets Society—Lago Vista
South Texas Animal Sanctuary—Weslaco
Southern Animal Rescue Association—Seguin
Special Pals Animal Shelter—Houston
St. John's Church & Retreat—Motgomery
StrayDog, Inc.—Dallas
Texas CARES—Dallas
Volunteers for Animal Protection—Kingwood

Utah

Best Friends Animal Sanctuary—Kanab
No More Homeless Pets Coalition in Utah—Salt Lake City
Community Animal Welfare Society (CAWS)—Salt Lake City

Vermont

Save Our Strays Association (SOS)—South Burlington

Virginia

Animal Adoption and Rescue Foundation—Richmond
Animal Aid Society—Hampton
Animal Allies—Fairfax Station
Animal Care New River Valley—Blacksburg
Animal Connections—Charlottesville
Animal Life RAFT (Rescue, Adopt, Foster & Transport) Ltd.—Quinton
Beath Animal Shelter—Dillwyn
Best Little Cat House in VA—Abingdon
Caring for Creatures Foundation—Palmyra
Cat Adoption and Rescue Efforts—Richmond
Central Virgina All-Breed Rescue—Fredericksburg
City Cat Adoptions—Richmond
Damien's Gift Feline Foundation—Troy
Fancy Cats Rescue Team—Herndon
For Love of Animals in Goochland (FLAG)—Manakin
Friends of Homeless Animals—Merrifield
Friends United with the Richmond Shelter FURS)—Richmond
Feline Foundation of Greater Washington—Merrifield

HAPPE (Homeless Animal Protection, Placement, Education)—Chesterfield
Hazen's Haven—Orange
HelpNtheBigDogs—Fluvanna County
Henrico Humane Society—Richmond
Hickory Hill K-9 Rescue—Ashland
Homeless Animals Rescue Team—Fairfax Station
K-9 New Life Center—Virginia Beach
League for Animal Protection—Fincastle
Lend A Paw—Falls Church
Meower Power Feral Cat Coalition—Chesapeake
Northern Virginia Animal League, Inc.—Manassas
Pet Assistance League of Virginia—Stafford
Pet Haven and Rescue—Falls Mills
Pet Rescue Foundation—Glen Allen, Richmond
Rappahannock Humane Society—Fredericksburg
Rescuing Animals in Need (RAIN)—Richmond
Richmond Animal League—Richmond
Rikki's Refuge—Orange
Sam's Haven—Lamplin
Second Chance Animal Shelter—Powhatan
Shamrock's Place—Midlothian
Shiloh Project—Fairfax
SOS (Save Our Shelters)—Richmond
Southside SPCA—Meherrin
SPCA of Northern Virginia—Arlington
Tazewell County Humane Society—Tazewell
The Humane Society of Montgomery County—Blacksburg
Whiskers-n-Wags Rescue Team, Inc.—Fredericksburg

Washington

Alternative Humane Society—Bellingham
Animal Home Find—Yakima
Animal Rescue Families—Bremerton
Benton-Franklin Humane Society—Pascoe
Cascade Animal Protection Society—Sumner
Cat Purebred Rescue—Seattle
Concern for Animals—Olympia
Dog Patch Humane—Colville
Friends of the Animals Foundation (FAF)—Seattle
Harbor Association of Volunteers for Animals—Westport
Hooterville Pets SafeHaus—Woodinville
Humane Society of Snohomish County—Arlington
Northwest Organization for Animal Help (NOAH)—Stanwood
Pasado's Safe Haven—Sultan
Progressive Animal Welfare Society (PAWS)—Lynnwood
Purrfect Pals—Arlington

Save Our Critters Society—Redondo
West Columbia Gorge Humane Society—Washouga

West Virginia
Cause for Paws—Harpers Ferry
Humane Society of North Central West Virginia—New Milton

Wisconsin
Adams County Humane Shelter—Friendship
Associated Society/Animal Protection—Sparta
Chequamegon Animal League—Ashland
Clark County Humane Society—Neillsville
Happy Endings No-Kill Shelter—Milwaukee
Hope Safe House—Racine
Kitty Connection—Milwaukee
Orphan Alley—Gresham
Richland Center Friends for Animals—Richland Center
Saint Francis Society No-Kill Shelter—Kenosha
Tri-County Animal Shelter & Adoption, Ltd.—Green Lake

Wyoming
Animal Care Center—Laramie
Casper Humane Society—Casper
St. Francis Animal Shelter, Inc.—Buffalo
The Lander Pet Connection—Lander
The Rock Springs Humane Society—Rock Springs

Canada
Animal Rescue Foundation—Calgary, Alberta
Animal Rescue Network—Montreal, Quebec
Fraser Valley Humane Society—Mission, British Columbia
Happy Cat Haven—Gibsons, British Columbia
Meow-Aid No-Kill Cat Shelter—Vancouver, British Columbia
Lethbridge District Humane Society—Lethbridge, Alberta
London Humane Society—London, Ontario
Ottawa Cat Rescue—Ottawa, Ontario
Pound Rescue Okotoks—Okotoks, Alberta
Street Cat Rescue—Saskatoon, Saskatchewan
The Animal Rescue Network of Montreal—Montreal, Quebec
Vancouver City Dog Pound—Vancouver, British Columbia

About the Author

The catchphrase for Randy Grim is "unlikely hero." For over a decade, Grim has been trying to call national attention to the scourge of abandoned, feral and wild street dogs. Now he is succeeding—in the national media, in legislatures, where others with more clout have failed or never tried at all. It takes an extra dose of real courage—Mark Twain's kind, the kind needed to act when you really are afraid—to mount daily rescue operations in some of this country's most dangerous streets. It takes an extra dose of courage for Grim even to publicize these dogs' world of misery. He is young and savvy, but crippled by panic attacks and phobias (of public places, parties, elevators, driving).

After rescuing his first street dog, Bonnie, he couldn't look away. "How can I?" he asks. "Each one says, *Don't leave me here*." And so the man who must pop Xanax to walk through an airport refuses to leave a starving, terror-stricken German Shepherd on a dark, icy and stormy East St. Louis street, even when a threatening tenement resident has him on the business end of a gun.

Likening his position to captain of a punctured life-raft, Grim rescues beaten, feral and wild city dogs from St. Louis's meanest streets. These are the untouchables, the dogs other shelters, many with multi-million-dollar budgets, call "irredeemable." To date, Grim has rescued over 5,000 street dogs, many suffering from gunshot wounds or amputations, others simply scared.

Grim is giving many of these dogs precisely what conventional wisdom and shelter management deem impossible: good endings. In just a few years, his lonely crusade has grown to 200 volunteers, 3 trappers, 10 rescue assistants, 5 cooperating veterinary clinics, 2 behaviorists, 2 no-kill shelters and 2 obedience trainers. And now, people are beginning to listen. To many, he's a hero. Working from within the brutal world and suffering of these dogs, Grim's work is ultimately uplifting. "One person counts," he says. And one person does. Grim's unwavering love for his dogs—for thousands of dogs throughout this country—has triumphed over public indifference and bone-chilling cruelty. People love Randy Grim. And they love his dogs.